THE MINORITY
CAREER GUIDE

DATE DUE

THE MINORITY CAREER GUIDE

WHAT AFRICAN AMERICANS, HISPANICS, AND ASIAN AMERICANS MUST KNOW TO SUCCEED IN CORPORATE AMERICA

MICHAEL F. KASTRE, NYDIA RODRIGUEZ KASTRE,
AND ALFRED G. EDWARDS

Peterson's
Princeton, NJ

Library of Congress Cataloging-in-Publication Data

Kastre, Michael F., 1946–
 The minority career guide : what African
Americans, Hispanics, and Asian Americans must
know to succeed in corporate America / Michael F.
Kastre, Nydia Rodriguez Kastre, and Alfred G.
Edwards.
  p. cm.
 ISBN 1-56079-258-2 (pbk.) : $12.95
 1. Vocational guidance for minorities—United
States. I. Kastre, Nydia Rodriguez, 1950– .
II. Edwards, Alfred G., 1949– . III. Title.
HF5382.5.U5K37 1993
331.7'02'08693—dc20   93-10668
                                 CIP

Cover and text design by Mike Freeland

Composition by Peterson's Guides

Printed in the United States of America

10 9 8 7 6 5 4

Acknowledgments

Some of the topics in this book were originally developed for the *National Business Employment Weekly.* I wish to express my appreciation to *NBEW* editors Tony Lee and Perri Capell for their encouragement and for allowing me, over the past several years, to develop and write about a range of career management issues.

I am also grateful to the editorial staff of the Career Communications Group of Baltimore for the opportunity to write about a broad cross-section of prominent minorities.

Finally, on behalf of my co-authors, I would like to thank editorial director James Gish of Peterson's for his keen insight and for giving us the opportunity to make this book a reality. His commitment and encouragement never wavered. And a special thanks to editor Kitty Colton for her skill and dedication in shaping the final product.

Michael F. Kastre

Contents

Foreword

Change in the American workplace, as in our society at large, is accelerating. Whole industries are realigning. Fierce global competition has become a reality for many corporations, necessitating increased productivity. Traditional jobs are being eliminated by the application of technology; new jobs requiring new skills and new perspectives are being created.

Shifting demographics are creating a new pool of minority talent that can help American corporations accommodate these fast-breaking changes. This means increased opportunities for minorities in the workplace. What has not changed, however, are the unique challenges and issues minorities will continue to face in the workplace.

The power and promise of a culturally diverse work force is just coming into focus. Although some progress has been made, much remains to be done. We owe it to ourselves to seize the initiative and build upon new opportunities.

Young minority professionals need to be prepared. That is where *The Minority Career Guide* can help. The authors have put together a book that covers career management from the unique perspective of minorities. *The Minority Career Guide* is not about how to eliminate discrimination. It *is* about how to overcome barriers and achieve professional excellence.

The book discusses what corporate America really wants, expects, and values; how to avoid traps that trip up too many minorities; how to plan alternate routes to success; and how to create a winning image. It provides you with the concrete experiences and advice of real people who have traveled the paths you wish to take. No one can do it for you, but *The Minority*

Career Guide will give you the basics for surviving and prospering in corporate America.

I can tell you from my personal experience that professional success is attainable when you have a dream and do the planning and preparing needed to make it a reality. Although I was raised in Birmingham, Alabama, at a time when opportunities were limited, I learned early that I could realize my goals by building a strong foundation, working hard, and using all the resources available to me.

I encourage you to be a dreamer, a planner, and a doer. Start building a strong foundation for your career today. If you are persistent and strive for excellence, you can achieve the success you want.

Carserlo Doyle
Manager of Telecommunications,
Baltimore Gas and Electric;
recipient of the 1993 Black Engineer
of the Year Award

Preface

THE AMERICAN RAINBOW

The power and promise of minorities is exerting a positive force on all aspects of the American scene—from politics to culture to the workplace. In the 1980s the Reverend Jesse Jackson coined the term "Rainbow Coalition" to describe minorities as a political entity. Yet as a young minority you are more than just part of an emerging political force; you are also integral to the future of the American economy and our ability to compete in a global marketplace.

African Americans, Hispanic Americans, and Asian Americans (people of the Far East, Southeast Asia, the Indian Subcontinent, and the Pacific Islands) are entering corporate America in droves. And though each culture and each individual is distinct, all have one common vision: the American dream of success. Making this dream a reality, however, requires planning and strategies to address the unique challenges and issues minorities face. This is especially true for young professionals, because you are faced with so many more possibilities and choices than your parents and grandparents were given.

Although it has a long way to go, corporate America is finally beginning to embrace cultural diversity. But it's up to you to recognize and seize the new opportunities at hand. Wanting to succeed is not enough; you must be armed with approaches that work. As a minority entering the work force or starting to shape your career, you're still bound to face a few potholes—in the form of bias and backward thinking—on the road to success. But with determination and savvy, you'll get there. From demystifying the new American workplace to helping you find your niche and plan for the future, *The Minority Career Guide* is dedicated to making your journey as smooth and rewarding as possible.

Chapter 1

CULTURAL DIVERSITY: THE NEW POWER IN THE WORK FORCE

Some career-management experts still say you'll never make it in main street corporate America if you are different. Don't believe them. Nowhere in American society is cultural diversity being felt more strongly than in the workplace. Although more progress needs to be made, many doors that were once locked to minorities are now being opened. But it's up to you to step inside and stake your claim.

What's at the root of this new awareness and acceptance of diversity? It hasn't happened overnight; rather, it's been a long, gradual process fueled by hard-fought battles and demographic realities.

THE FIGHT FOR EQUAL OPPORTUNITY

Civil rights and equal opportunity have been intertwined since the push for equality began, and the fight has produced results thanks to powerful leadership and landmark legislation.

In 1941 President Franklin D. Roosevelt encouraged minority employment by ordering defense contractors to cease discriminatory hiring practices. The next major step came in 1953, when President Dwight D. Eisenhower created a committee to hear complaints about job discrimination involving federal contracts. Still, at this point no one was being punished for non-compliance.

> **Minority workers can no longer be force-fitted into the traditional company mold.**

In 1961, as the fight against segregation continued to intensify behind the leadership of Martin Luther King Jr., President John F. Kennedy introduced the term *affirmative action*. The president began putting teeth into minority hiring rules for government contractors by creating a commission to investigate contractors' practices, imposing sanctions for noncompliance, and collecting employment statistics.

In 1963 a racially mixed crowd of 200,000 rallied in Washington, D.C., to hear Dr. King deliver his "I have a dream" speech. After President Kennedy's assassination that year, his successor, Lyndon Johnson, took up the fight for equal opportunity. The culmination of these efforts was the 1964 Civil Rights Act, which banned all discrimination in voting, jobs, and public accommodations. A year after Congress passed the Civil Rights Act, President Johnson issued an order requiring companies that do business with the government to put affirmative-action plans in writing.

The Equal Employment Opportunity Commission was created by Congress to enforce Title VII of the Civil Rights Act, which prohibits discrimination based on race, color, religion, sex, or national origin. Although you can't legislate complete fairness and equality, the EEOC does have teeth. Its five commissioners and a general counsel, appointed by the president, have the power to make equal employment opportunity policy and enforce federal laws prohibiting employee discrimination. In addition to investigation and litigation, their methods include conciliation, coordination, education, and technical assistance.

The Power of the Law

Title VII touches virtually all corners of the workplace. It covers private employers, federal, state, and local governments, and educational institutions that have 15 or more employees. Private and public employment agencies, labor organizations, and joint labor-management committees for apprenticeship and training also must abide by the law. Title VII states that it is illegal to discriminate in hiring and firing; compensation, assignment, or classification of employees; transfer, promotion, layoff, or recall; job advertisements; recruitment; testing; use of company facilities; training and apprenticeship programs; fringe benefits; pay, retirement plans, and disability leave; or other terms and conditions of employment.

The law covers the full spectrum of issues, some of which you may have never considered. For example, it states that citizenship requirements, preferences, or rules requiring employees to be fluent in English or to speak only English may be unlawful if they disproportionately exclude individuals of a particular national origin and are not justified by business necessity.

THE NUMBERS GAME

For American corporations today, enacting affirmative-action policies and accommodating cultural diversity are no longer just social objectives legislated by law; they are business priorities and necessities.

More than at any time in our history, shifting demographics are dramatically altering the structure of the work force. Minorities made up 22 percent of the labor market in 1992; as a minority, you are part of a tidal wave that is beginning to wash over corporate America. Of the 55.8 million workers expected to enter the work force between the years 1990 and 2005, 19 million, or fully one third, will be either African American (7.2 million), Hispanic (8.8 million), or Asian American (3.4 million), according to U.S. Department of Labor statistics.

Faced with this vast influx, businesses are discovering that minority workers can no longer be force-fitted into the traditional company mold. They're also realizing that minorities are a vital resource in the emerging global economy. With a diverse work force, companies are better prepared to capitalize on the newly diverse marketplace.

A Change for the Better

In their scramble to adapt to the country's sweeping demographic, social, and legal changes, the vast majority of Fortune 500 companies, and thousands of smaller firms, have established programs to deal with cultural diversity in the workplace. What they are discovering, however, is that diversity engenders far more promise than problems.

Why did it take companies so long to wake up to the power of diversity? Fear of change—and, in some cases, racism—is at the heart of it. If legislation and population shifts hadn't necessitated a new approach, minorities might still be shut out of American corporations today, simply because corporate

America is a very conservative place. Change and difference are scary words to those who worship the status quo.

Fortunately, change *is* forcing its way into the workplace, and corporations are learning to work with it and see it as a positive. In 1966 only about 4 percent of all managers and professionals in U.S. companies were African American. Today that number has climbed to over 16 percent, according to Bureau of Labor statistics. More progress needs to be made, but as one General Motors manager puts it, "the bottom line is companies are learning that we don't have to be the same in order to work together." Executives are finding that they can achieve common goals and objectives within the framework of diversity. And it's finally becoming clear that differences can be assets, not drawbacks. Minority workers are proving that a variety of viewpoints and backgrounds leads to new ideas and new solutions.

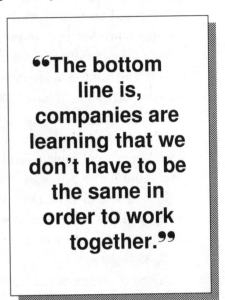

"The bottom line is, companies are learning that we don't have to be the same in order to work together."

The New Role of the Diversity Manager

Many corporations view diversity as a business necessity. Programs that address cultural diversity include those to attract, train, and retain minority workers. "If you don't have a work force that reflects your customers, you are not going to be competitive," says Yvonne Alverio, director of work force diversity at the Aetna Insurance Company. "For that reason, [diversity training] is often tied to a company's business plan."

Alverio is one of a new breed of managers whose job is to develop and sponsor workshops and seminars that help workers become more sensitive to each other and respectful of their differences; work with recruiters and affirmative-action officers to recruit and train a wide cross-section of workers who reflect the company's client base; and make sure the company is abiding by EEO regulations.

"We have diversity training for virtually every employee," says Xerox spokesman Judd Everhart. "It's done at different levels and using different approaches. New-employee training is 40 hours, and it includes diversity. We even have a theater group that comes in and does miniplays about situations that might occur in the workplace. Afterward there is a half-hour discussion period."

The commitment that nurtures such sensitivity starts at the top of an organization. Today, most large companies have formalized their commitment to cultural diversity. Xerox policy, for example, states:

At Xerox, we view diversity as something more than a moral imperative or a business necessity—we see it as a business opportunity. For us, diversity goes beyond numbers and targets; it is the acceptance and celebration of people of all ages with globally diverse backgrounds who bring fresh new ideas, opinions, perspectives, and borderless creativity that enrich the lives of others. Diversity is a global mosaic—a tapestry filled with exciting colors, shapes, designs, and accents.

(reprinted with permission of the Xerox Corporation)

The giant corporation sees work force diversity as an evolution from equal employment opportunity initiatives in the 1960s and aggressive affirmative action in the 70s to a balanced strategy for the 90s and beyond. This means more than improved hiring practices. It's giving them the opportunity to rise into management positions.

Making It Work for You

Unfortunately, while corporations are changing their policies, many individuals haven't changed their private biases to adapt to the new diversity in the workplace. On a personal level, some businesspeople, especially managers and executives, still see minorities as an unknown, and perhaps somewhat threatening, quantity.

What this means is that, despite all the new opportunities out there, you're still going to have to prove yourself in the workplace. You need to show corporate America that you understand what it wants and that you are able to deliver.

Every corporation is like a separate nation, with its own language and its own rules, both written and unwritten. Succeeding involves learning the rules and playing by them, and that starts even before you land your first job. It comes down to being prepared: Before you walk through that open doorway, you need to know who you are, what you're stepping into and what you're hoping to find.

Chapter 2

TAKING STOCK AND SETTING GOALS

The answer to the question "What is the most common failure of young minority professionals when trying to plan their careers?" might surprise you. When asked, successful mid- and senior-level minority executives point to what one Hispanic businessman labels "potluck planning." He says, "As minorities we are so used to not having a full range of favorable choices that we tend to seize either the first or the wrong opportunity. Whatever turns up too often decides the direction of our professional lives."

He further observes, "We [minorities] often display poor planning skills because we haven't been trained to do this like nonminorities. For example, in the corporate world it is managers and executives who plan and set goals. Since we have been traditionally underrepresented in these positions, we lack planning experience." He advises young minority professionals to "adopt a nonminority approach to assessing and packaging both short- and long-term needs, objectives, and skills. Corporate structures and available career paths are still dominated by traditional nonminorities," he says. "If you don't think along these lines, you won't be able to match up your goals or agenda to what's available."

Because of upheavals across the corporate landscape, long-term planning now is trickier than ever. No matter: You don't have to let fate deal the cards. People have long pondered, "Is this what I want to do for the rest of my life?" In today's environment you may have to adjust planning times by not trying to forecast as far. For instance, given the business climate likely to exist in the 1990s, five years in a particular industry or career may be a lifetime.

> **Many of us are so busy peering out that we never take the time to look inward.**

There is not just one perfect place out there for you; there are many. Before you can find one that suits you, however, you need to find yourself. Prior to writing your resume and starting your search, you need to know who you are and what type of job you are looking for, in what field. Consider the following factors:

- **Type of work**—What do you enjoy or want to do?

- **Social and family needs**—Are such things as child- and elder-care important to you?

- **Money**—How much do you need or want?

- **Prestige**—Do you want or need it? How much is enough?

- **Security**—Is it important to you? It's usually less so for singles than for those with dependent families.

- **Independence**—Do you enjoy working with a minimum of structure? For example, would you be happier working in outside sales or as part of a corporate marketing team?

- **Travel**—Do you enjoy being on the road or prefer to stay close to home?

- **Contact with others**—Do you enjoy a lot of interaction with the public or are you content to stay in the office?

- **Competition and pressure**—Do you thrive on pressure? For example, would you enjoy working in a high-powered sales group? Or would you prefer something a little less stressful?

If you are already working and are thinking about changing jobs, some of the questions you need answers to, in addition to those listed above, are:

- **What do I like best about my present work?**

- **What job-related tasks do I perform best?** (These are generally the ones you like the best.)

- **What transferable skills do I possess and use on the job?**

- **What do I dislike about my present job?**

ROADBLOCKS

Choosing not to set career goals puts you at the mercy of other people and events. Yet for most people, setting long-term goals ranks right up there with cleaning out their closets. This reluctance is reinforced by false assumptions including:

- **The right career path and moves will reveal themselves when the time is right.** This "lightning will strike" mentality doesn't work. Without goals or a plan you are likely to drift along on rough water or be beached on corporate low tides.

- **Planning will stunt my creativity and block potential opportunities.** Nothing could be further from the truth.

You're the driver. You have to set the course because if you don't know where you're going, you'll surely end up somewhere else. And this destination may not be very desirable.

- **There's no point in setting goals and planning when the economy's so uncertain. I may not even be able to get a job.** If you don't plan, you have just greatly increased the odds that your worst fears will come true.

- **I'm competing with lots of others trying to achieve the same goals. What's the use of trying to plan when so much is beyond my control?** Never kid yourself; opportunities are out there. But too many of us don't recognize them because they are usually disguised as hard work.

- **Others will take care of me.** Don't count on it. If your "champion" doesn't plan, he or she may not even be around to help you.

Goal-setting carries a reward: an increased chance of success. But it requires commitment and discipline. Neglecting to take time to plan is easy when you are locked into the daily struggle most of us fight to just maintain our normal lives. But it must be done.

One of the most effective ways to make the time and formalize the process is to make an appointment with yourself. Even a couple of hours every three to six months can be sufficient to plan and review results.

DISCOVER THE REAL YOU

Being hungry for success and its rewards is essential for ambitious career-builders. But as one successful minority executive warns, "Career aspirations too often blind us to our own aptitudes, likes, and dislikes. Honest self-evaluation is always the best remedy."

Have an Out-of-Body Experience

You should create and define the roles you want in your professional life. This self-assessment process is not that difficult if you follow some basics. We have all heard of people who have reported "leaving their bodies" when they suffered great trauma. Yours doesn't have to be a painful experience, but it can be helpful to get outside yourself. This is a lot like daydreaming, only tempered with realism. You must see your blemishes and warts along with your strengths. It's not a pass-or-fail situation, but rather a frank assessment of who you are and where you want to be.

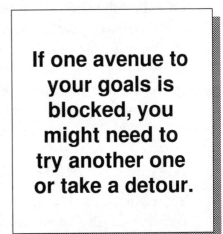

If one avenue to your goals is blocked, you might need to try another one or take a detour.

Find a quiet time and place. Get a pad of paper and a pen. Unplug the phone. Sit back in a comfortable chair. Start asking yourself some questions. Who are you looking at? Are you a people person? Are you driven by power and money or job satisfaction?

Once you start this questioning, you may find yourself answering, "I don't know." Many of us are so busy peering out that we never take the time to look inward.

It's easy to say that you like advertising, engineering, or whatever. You have to go further. For example, suppose advertising is your chosen field. Do you have a product or industry preference? Do you want to be an advertising manager for a small company or an executive for a major corporation?

Be honest and thorough. What do you really like to do? What type of work do you want to perform? What types of organizations or industries attract you? What are you good at? What training or experience can you offer? Where do you ultimately envision yourself? What areas will you need to improve to make it? Which of your skills are transferable—that is, not job-specific? If you have trained to become an accountant, for example, you could just as easily perform financial functions for a computer company as for a hospital.

Write down your answers, along with any other factors that are important to you. Then study your list and refine it. It's really a picture—a self-portrait. You are going to need the answers to identify specific goals and target particular types of industries, jobs, and promotional opportunities.

SCORE WITH GOALS

You have assets. Use them to achieve your goals. Based on your personality, qualifications, and expected growth, write down what you want to achieve. Make sure you understand what it takes to get there. Start with short-term objectives. For instance, maybe you want to become an operations manager within two years. Perhaps you want to be the supervisor of an accounting department. Or maybe you have your sights set on earning an M.B.A. at night school.

Next, think about where you want to be further down the line. Perhaps you'd like to be the vice president of manufacturing or product development. Maybe you'd like to be a consultant or president of your own company.

Once you've formulated a set of goals, write them down. Seeing them in black and white gives them reality. Next, classify all of your goals into three categories:

1. no-compromise, must-have
2. important but nonessential
3. nice to have

Now, for every goal you've established, list an alternate goal. (Since we don't live in an ideal world, you should always have backup plans.)

Great Expectations

When setting goals, remember to temper them with realism. It's great to shoot for the moon—but for that you need a rocket ship. In other words, you can achieve whatever you want, as long as you have the right skills and qualifications. If your career expectations greatly exceed your capabilities, you have a problem. On the other hand, once you have realistic goals in place, all you need to get moving is a plan of action to achieve them. Without a well-thought-out plan, reaching your destination is almost impossible.

PLANNING FOR SUCCESS

Some plans only last a couple of months. Others may extend several years. But once you have a good plan, either short- or long-term, making decisions will be much easier. In a column next to your goals, jot down what you feel you need or must do to achieve them. Try to set deadlines for yourself.

After you have finished your self-evaluation, set it aside for one week. Then go back and see if your goals and plans still make sense. Discuss them with someone whose judgment you trust and respect. A person who knows you well might be able to make constructive suggestions or point out any areas you may have overlooked.

It's Not Cast In Concrete

Periodically monitor and adjust your strategies to fit your needs and situation. Some changes in plans are caused by basic changes in goals; others are simply new approaches to reach the same objective. Just as a map contains many roads, if one avenue to your goals is blocked, you might need to try another or take a detour.

Also, industries, people, and work situations change. For example, you might outgrow your perfect position. Or your office might face severe budget cuts. Perhaps your boss will move on, leaving an intolerable idiot in charge. You have to be smart enough to move with the times. A flexible, easy-to-follow plan of action will ensure that you can always adapt to circumstances and continue to survive, succeed, and enjoy job satisfaction.

ANDRE'S ODYSSEY

From his high school days in Buffalo, New York, when he attended his first lab class, Andre wanted to be a biologist. His long-term goals were fuzzy, but in the back of his mind, he saw himself working his way up the technical ladder at a prominent laboratory. After graduating from college, Andre went to

Washington, D.C., to work in a government health laboratory. He hated it. Not the organization, but his job.

Over the next two years he transferred to several different departments, but he just wasn't satisfied. Deciding that he needed a change, he accepted a position in Minnesota. But he continued to find something lacking in his work, and he felt isolated and even more miserable in a new city. He quit and moved to the Northeast to live with his sister and her husband.

At age 28, after several more jobs, he decided it was time to figure out what was wrong. After all, he had enjoyed biology in school. Somehow, though, that didn't translate into job satisfaction. He knew he liked the laboratory environment, but perhaps he didn't really like his specific field.

Still unsure, he started taking some courses at a local university. After one semester he found himself drawn to business administration. While he continued to pursue his new interest at school during the evening, he was offered a job as the administrative officer for a large research laboratory. He enjoyed it; the job enabled him to combine his new skills with his understanding of the way scientific laboratories operate.

"Suddenly I was able to combine my likes and skills for the best of all possible worlds," Andre says. He admits he was lucky to find his niche and says that self-assessment and planning would have saved him time and energy. "Whether your career path is on track or not, you should keep defining goals and developing plans to accomplish them," he says. "I know I wish I had done this early on. Keep monitoring your progress and where you are headed. Don't be afraid to make changes. You can save yourself a lot of frustration and wasted effort."

Don't fool yourself. When you know you don't like what you're doing, don't just hope it will get better; take action.

KRISTI SCALES THE WALL

Kristi migrated to Los Angeles from Korea when she was 22 years old. When she arrived, she had already earned the equivalent of a bachelor's degree in computer science, but she knew virtually no English. She studied for several months at a local community college, trying to grasp the language just well enough to get a job. Finally, she found work as a programmer with a company that produced financial management information systems for medical facilities.

Kristi thoroughly enjoyed working with software, and the company was pleased with her efforts. However, because of her poor language skills, she was basically put in the corner to write code. Others worked with clients to define system requirements and install software in hospitals and clinics.

For the first year it didn't bother Kristi to see her co-workers, many with less technical knowledge than she had, receive promotions into team leader and management roles. Gradually, though, this began to bother her. So she started to aggressively pursue management opportunities. "I wasn't taken seriously," she says. "Each time I tried, I felt like I was being patted on the head like a child and dismissed."

Desperate to change the situation, she sat down at home one evening and wrote her goals on a piece of paper. Next to each goal she listed the qualifications she'd need to reach it. She then tried to match up her strengths—her computer skills—with the requirements. They were clearly not sufficient.

She started another list. "I was all too painfully aware of my weaknesses, but I wrote them down anyway," she recalls. From her observations at work she knew that she lacked not only strong language skills but also management abilities. She had seen others making presentations to customers, developing schedules and management plans, and talking to the boss about time-sheet financial charge numbers needed to bill labor hours for their staff.

For several weeks she studied her lists. "The obvious didn't really strike me at first," she says. "Then it became clear: I had to improve my language and management skills. It seemed like an impossible task, and I was depressed because I thought it would take a long time. I guess I was in a hurry. But I had no choice but to start the process."

Based on her goals, job requirements, strengths, and weaknesses, Kristi made a plan. She started taking English courses. She enrolled in a public-speaking class. She refused to speak Korean with her friends, even during class breaks. She studied management books. She continued to work hard but kept quiet on the job.

Her big break came almost a year later. Her team leader was out sick with the flu, and there was a major presentation to be made. Kristi went to the boss and convinced her that she could make the briefing. The boss, who had noticed an improvement in Kristi's verbal skills, reluctantly agreed.

Kristi gave an excellent presentation, and the rest is history. She has since left the company and now heads up information systems for a major southern California hospital group. She also finds time to preach the power of goal-setting and planning to others in the Korean community.

Taking stock is the first part of a layered strategy. Once you really know your goals, your strengths, and your weaknesses, you are ready to start the job hunt.

Chapter 3

THE HUNT: LAUNCHING A SUCCESSFUL JOB SEARCH

Your education, experience, skills, and personality define you—the product. The focus of your search is to find the right buyer who is willing to pay for this.

How fast you succeed will be determined by how aggressively you market yourself, how realistically you price yourself, economic conditions, and competition from others. If you are not employed, marketing yourself should be a full-time job. That means spending a minimum of 40 hours a week working on every aspect of the search. If you are currently working but desire a change, you need to devote as much free time as possible to your effort.

Although others might help, no one is going to do it for you. While getting the right job may be your top priority, it is probably not going to keep your colleagues, friends, or neighbors awake at night. But if you approach the hunt with enthusiasm, optimism, and realistic expectations, you will succeed.

AIM AT THE RIGHT TARGET

Before you start out, you have to make sure you are pointed in the right direction. The shotgun approach can work, but a well-focused search can save time and energy and yield more satis-fying results.

Define Your Bull's-Eye

You may say, "I'm open to anything." But if you adopt this position, you might find yourself wasting a great deal of energy trying to cover too much territory. Why bother? After all, you have a good idea of what you want because you've already taken stock and set goals (if you read Chapter 2, that is). Pull out your list and review what's important to you. When consid-ering potential workplaces, you'll also want to consider the fol-lowing criteria:

- **Size**—Smaller organizations often represent the opportu-nity for you to wear more hats. For example, if you are an engineer, you may be a project leader, a head of quality, and a customer service representative. Smaller companies may also offer more growth opportunity as new positions open up. Larger firms may offer a broader product line, more formal training programs, and the chance to special-ize. What you choose will depend on your personal goals and work preferences.

- **Industry**—Consider your preferences for a particular type of business. If, however, economic times are tight, you may want to expand your search to related industries.

- **Location**—You need to decide where you physically want to be: in a large city, close to a major metropolitan area, or in a smaller town. One note of caution: If you select a target that's outside your geographic area, you may end up paying travel expenses for interviews unless you are a renowned whiz or possess skills that are in demand.

- **Corporate culture**—It's reflected in everything from office environments and corporate social activities to dress codes. For example, you might want to work in a private office, but the ABC Corporation places dozens of young professionals in a large, open work space. When you talk to others during your search, you will discover which organizations offer more informal versus more formal ways of doing business. You will need to evaluate which corporate personality traits are important to you.

A SNAPSHOT OF THE EMERGING AMERICAN COMPANY

Before you start your job search, you need to know the lay of the corporate landscape: what's hot (and what will be a few years from now), what's not, and where the jobs are.

Among the trends that will mark corporate America in the 1990s are:

- increased emphasis not only on productivity, but quality and variety
- increased flexibility to provide products and services
- the rise of information as a product
- increased employee empowerment
- smaller business units
- increased awareness of cultural diversity as a means to bring new ideas and innovation into the workplace
- increased awareness of global competition
- more cooperative corporate ventures

- a move toward specialized high-tech corridors
- a shift from downtown to suburbia and beyond
- significant growth in small companies
- less visible (but still flourishing) "old boy" networks
- reduced benefits, such as retirement guarantees
- less job security

Hot Spots

Emerging hot spots and the technology that is making them sizzle include:

- Corning, New York—ceramics, electronics packaging
- Princeton, New Jersey—biotechnology, telecommunications
- Philadelphia—medical technology, biotechnology
- Baltimore/Washington/Northern Virginia—medical technology, software, systems integration, imaging
- Orlando/Central Florida—electro-optics, lasers, computer technology
- Minneapolis/St. Paul—medical instruments
- Austin, Texas—computer technology
- Richardson, Texas—telecommunications systems
- Boise, Idaho—electronic chips, laser printers
- Salt Lake City—medical technology
- Provo, Utah—software development
- San Diego—biotechnology and communications
- San Francisco Bay area—biotechnology
- Tucson—lasers and electro-optics

Most of these explosive growth areas are located near major academic centers. American industry, long faulted for weak research and development efforts, is finally beginning to recognize the power of university research and development facilities and laboratories. Universities have the technical specialties, and often the facilities and companies supply much-needed capital and vision. These new relationships are not only fueling growth at major corporations but are also powering many small companies, which are challenging the giants in everything from computers and communications to lasers and medical breakthroughs.

Urban areas will retain their role as magnets for companies, but there is a definite shift from downtown to suburbia and beyond. Because of this shift, today's young professionals need to broaden their geographic view of potential employers.

> **Associations can be the single biggest gold mine for young professionals seeking information.**

Growth Areas

Although nobody has a crystal ball, these key sectors and industries promise to shape this decade and heat up demand for those who can contribute:

- Health care
- Environmental services
- Genetics and biomedicine
- Information systems
- Training and education

- Construction (related to infrastructure such as roads, bridges, and water-treatment systems)
- Computers and communications (especially related networks and software)

All of these industries have human resource needs that cut across technical specialties and require a broad spectrum of professionals. For instance, health care is more than just medical doctors and nurses; it also encompasses accountants, administrators, trainers, and a whole range of other disciplines.

Also be aware of potential soft spots in the workplace. Sectors and related industries that have lost their sizzle include:

- Defense
- Aerospace
- Automobile manufacturing
- Banks and financial institutions
- Government, especially state and local

ALTERNATE ROUTES AND HIDDEN OPPORTUNITIES

Minorities often overlook opportunities offered by smaller and lesser-known businesses. Fortune 500 companies conjure up images of fat corporate expense accounts, first-class air travel, and glass-tower offices. Such companies get more press, have better name recognition, may recruit more heavily on college campuses, and may have larger concentrations of minorities. At first glance, their numbers seem to indicate more employment opportunities.

Yet in truth, small business is the backbone of the U.S. economy. From 1989 through 1991, companies employing fewer than 500 workers were responsible for adding all the net new jobs in America, according to statistics from the U.S. Department of Labor. Over 80 percent of all American workers are employed by companies with fewer than 1,000 people. Of that group, a full two thirds work for firms with fewer than 100 employees.

To be sure, big companies are important. They still hire thousands of employees annually. But the portrait of corporate America is not that of a giant. Minorities need to discover these small organizations and tap into them as a potential source of employment.

The Business of Government

Don't neglect to investigate the specialized niche offered by the federal government. Uncle Sam is the largest employer in the country. The government offers an unparalleled variety of career opportunities, filling thousands of jobs annually in a range of occupations. Since the federal government is not a single unit, but rather hundreds of different organizations, the place to start is with the U.S. Office of Personnel Management. Consult your local telephone directory for the nearest regional or area office of the OPM for requirements and information.

Shipping Out

Most of us never explore all the corners of the United States. Still, many young professionals dream of living and working overseas. It takes a certain type of person to work abroad; strong language skills and adaptability are important. Be sure to thoroughly research the country you're interested in, the types of jobs available, and the legal and logistical details of living and working there. Try calling the nearest foreign embassy for your target country; it can provide lots of helpful information. Also, check the library for books on living and working abroad. Locating and talking to someone who lives in, or has lived in, the country will definitely help ease the transition.

Internships

Although not for everyone, internships can give valuable experience to college students and professionals just entering the work force. They often lead to the development of marketable skills that will come in very handy down the road.

Temporary or Contract Employment

We've all heard of companies "downsizing"; today the term *outsourcing* is becoming equally common as companies contract whole corporate functions to outside organizations or individuals. What this means is that more and more workers are being hired on a contingent or contract basis, hired temporarily to do a job that might last anywhere from a day to over a year.

From 1982 to 1992, temporary employment increased almost 250 percent, while all employment grew less than 20 percent. By the year 2000, contingent or contract workers are expected to make up half the labor force, according to Department of Labor statistics. The majority of these workers are not professionals, but a growing number are.

You can land a temporary job through an agency that specializes in these types of jobs (see later in this chapter for more information on temporary agencies) or as a free-lance professional who contracts independently with companies.

BE A SPY

Never start your job search without first arming yourself with facts. Research is critical. Fortunately, the amount of information available on corporate America is staggering. With a telephone and public libraries, you can spy on anyone in business. The right information enables you to:

- aim at the right targets
- customize your resume
- network effectively, including tapping into nonminority networks
- perform effectively at interviews (as you will see in Chapter 5)

Libraries

Start your investigations by taking a trip to the local public library. If you are unfamiliar with research techniques or your digging skills are rusty, go straight to the reference desk. The vast majority of reference librarians are not only extremely knowledgeable but genuinely like to help people.

With publications like *Standard & Poor's Register* and *Ward's Directory of the Largest U.S. Corporations*, you can determine company size, location, and sales numbers. Such resources as the *Wall Street Journal Index* can provide you with timely articles about companies and industry trends. Another helpful reference book is the *Reader's Guide to Periodical Literature*, which lists recent articles about specific areas, professions, and industries. After a couple of searches, you'll be able to profile a company in very little time.

Annual Reports

These are usually available from an organization's public relations office. (If the company is very small, you may have to settle for corporate capability brochures and similar literature.) An annual report provides a complete overview of the company, including corporate goals and philosophy, services and products, organization, operating divisions, location, sales, and history.

Trade Associations

There is an association for almost every industry and profession in the corporate landscape. Many publish journals and newsletters. Associations and other types of professional groups can be the single biggest gold mine for young job seekers. A good source for learning who's out there is Gale Research's *Encyclopedia of Associations*. (Also see the Appendix for selected groups and associations.)

When performing research, write down pertinent information. Organize it clearly. Remember, research is a key ingredient of every element of your search and interview activities, so don't shortchange it. If you do, you may be seriously hurting your career.

THE ROAD TO YOUR FUTURE

You can take many paths to your career destination. Which one you choose will depend on your situation, but don't ignore any of the possibilities. Those most frequently traveled are:

- Networks
- Trade associations and societies

- Direct application
- Newspaper/trade journal advertisements
- Employment/placement agencies
- Job fairs
- Temporary agencies

Networks That Work

Estimates vary, but most industry professionals agree that networking accounts for the filling of over 50 percent of all positions. But it's not magic. As powerful and effective as networks can be, there's no trick to landing on your feet in the right place at the right time. It's a matter of preparation, planning, and persistence. What you're doing when you network is sowing seeds. And that's what produces impressive results.

For centuries people have been hitting up friends, neighbors, former classmates, and relatives for jobs or for information that might lead to them. Whether they realized it or not, they were engaging in a crude form of networking. For your purposes, though, you need to formalize such efforts into a well-organized campaign.

The name of the game is people contact. Don't think of networking as "using" others but rather as gaining access to a people data base. When approached, most people will understand because most of them have been there themselves.

"I never used to take calls from friends or acquaintances too seriously when they got in touch trying to get a lead on a job," says Helen, a systems analyst in Portland. "Oh, sure, if it was convenient and I could think of something off the top of my head I would help. But then," she continues, "I lost *my* job, and the shoe was on the other foot." Now, she admits, "I will never again take such a call lightly. I know what it's like to pick up the phone and hold your breath, hoping that perhaps this could be the call that sends you on your way."

The Instant Network

Start with your inner circle and work your way out. Make a list of family members, former classmates, teachers, colleagues or acquaintances from professional associations (if you're already started in your career), and people you've met through clubs and religious groups who might be able to help. Everyone you've ever come in contact with is a potential link in your network.

Perhaps you have a small family or a limited circle of acquaintances. Don't despair. Cold calling can also produce the backbone of a network. You're a spy, remember?

You can find the names of people to contact in business journals and directories, through associations (these can be especially helpful and informative—see the appendix for a list of key organizations), annual reports, and a variety of other sources. Once you've got some names, it's time to activate your network.

Network Basics

There are two ways to operate your network—the spoken word and the written word. The first is the most common. If you network as vigorously as you should, your telephone is going to become an extension of your ear. Your goal is to:

- let people know you are available
- discover hidden openings

- increase your knowledge of what's required by organizations
- hone your interview skills

You've already started making a list. Expand it to include not only the name of your contact but his or her title, company, address, and secretary's name. Beside these write what you hope to gain from the contact.

When you call someone you know, your conversation might sound like this:

> Unless you want to limit your career opportunities to minority companies, you must tap into nonminority networks.

Donna: "Hi, Frank, how are you? It's been over a year since we attended that job fair together in Chicago."

Frank: "I remember. Did you end up taking that job at XYZ Corporation?"

Donna: "Yes, and I was there until last month. ABC Company bought us out, and I was caught in a restructuring."

Frank: "I'm sorry to hear that. What are your plans?"

Donna: "I'm just starting to look at my options. Do you know any companies that are expanding their operations?..."

You get the idea. Donna isn't pressuring Frank by asking for a job. She's probing and asking for advice. Your contact may be willing to steer you in the right direction if he or she knows of an opening.

Contacting people by phone is almost always better because

it is faster and more direct. But a letter can also be effective. For example, Donna might have written something like this:

> Dear Frank,
>
> I hope things are going well for you.
>
> It's been over a year since we attended the Computer Job Fair in Chicago. I ended up taking that job with XYZ Corporation. Unfortunately, the company was bought by ABC, and I was caught in a massive restructuring in the wake of the takeover. But my computer programming skills are highly transferable to other sectors, and I am confident that I can find an organization where I can put my experience to good use.
>
> Frank, I'm seeking your advice and information to help me locate an expanding organization that might be able to use my skills. I realize that this is a hectic time of the year, but I'll give you a call in a few days to see if we can't set up a brief meeting. I'm looking forward to seeing you.

If a friend has referred you to someone you don't know, a phone conversation might go something like this:

> "Hello, Mr. Jones? My name is Donna Rivera. We don't know each other, but a mutual friend, Frank Smith, suggested I call. XYZ Corporation was recently bought out, and I was caught in the subsequent restructuring. Since my programming skills are highly transferable, I'm seeking advice and information to locate an expanding organization in

the environmental services industry where my skills might fit...."

Use a similar technique for cold calls (when you don't know the person and have no contact in common). The key is to be concise, composed, straightforward, and polite. For instance:

> "Hello, Mr. Jones? My name is Donna Rivera. We don't know each other, but I'm calling to see if I might get some help. XYZ Corporation was recently bought out, and I was caught in the subsequent restructuring. I'm a computer programmer, and a number of my colleagues have suggested that my experience might fit well in the environmental services industry. I've been doing some informal networking with people in this field to try to identify any organization that might be expanding and have need for xx programming skills...."

You are trying to establish a friendly dialogue. While the door won't always open, it will often enough to help you develop new contacts and leads.

Nonminority Networks

The single biggest disadvantage minorities face when trying to find a job, move around within an industry, or break into a new field is that far too many operate in exclusive minority networks. Unless you want to limit your career opportunities, you must tap into nonminority networks.

Don't shut yourself out of the majority of openings and

career opportunities that are out there. Here's how to integrate your network:

- Go out of your way to join community activities where the majority are nonminorities. Volunteer as much time as you can spare.
- Attend speakers' bureaus, workshops, and seminars in which most participants are nonminorities.
- When cold-calling, target organizations with large numbers of nonminorities.
- Go back and look up former classmates or co-workers who are nonminorities and reestablish the lines of communications.
- Include nonminorities on your guest list for social occasions.
- Never overlook *any* opportunity to expand your circle.

Not all nonminorities are going to welcome you with open arms. But if you are professional and persistent, the majority will. The fact that a handful of nonminorities have an attitude problem doesn't mean you should. There are a lot of real people out there who might be able to help you—if not now, then perhaps in the future.

Networking Dos and Don'ts

Develop the ability to use, not abuse, your network. At first, as you activate your network, you may make some mistakes. For example, conversations may not always go smoothly. Don't let it bother you; it happens to everybody. Shrug it off and go on. However, there are some very important networking dos and don'ts.

Do:

- remember to identify your skills
- state your job or career objective
- express yourself clearly
- find common ground and pursue it
- seek advice and be a good listener
- keep appointments and promises
- express your appreciation for the contact's time and advice. If he or she was extremely helpful, you might even write a short thank-you note. This can also serve as a good reminder if the contact promised to get back to you with some information.
- follow through and stay in touch with people

Don't:

- ask for a job. You're simply seeking suggestions and advice.
- be bitter or bad-mouth others
- push too hard. Putting pressure on others usually turns them off.
- contact a person too frequently. Pestering someone will not produce results.

Trade Associations and Societies

The power of professional groups was discussed earlier. In addition to being great sources of information, some offer placement services. Always contact associations that represent your profession or industry. You might be pleasantly surprised at the doors they can open.

Direct Application

You can compile a list of target companies and send a cold-call cover letter and resume to them. If you do, make sure you do your homework first so you can address the letter to a specific person, preferably a department head or line manager rather than the personnel manager.

Newspaper/Trade Journal Advertisements

Scanning the employment ads in newspapers or journals can be effective, but you have to move fast because such announcements can generate hundreds of replies. Always include a cover letter with your resume. If the ad mentions a fax number, use it.

Employment/Placement Agencies

These groups are also known as "headhunters." But before hiring someone to find you a job, know what you are getting into. These are the most common commercial agencies:

- **Employment agencies** work to find jobs for candidates and also usually offer resume-writing assistance. Either you or the organization that hires you pays a fee for the agency's services.
- **Search firms** custom recruit and locate candidates with specific talents and skills for corporate clients. They may be paid a retainer by the company, or they may be paid after they deliver. In either case, you should never pay anything to deal with them.
- **Outplacement agencies** conduct job searches for displaced workers. Usually the fees for these firms are paid by the company trying to relocate the employee.

However, these agencies also offer private outplacement services for which the individual pays, usually up front.

Have It Your Way: Agency Basics

- **Don't allow agencies to put you on the interview treadmill.** Some agencies will set up numerous interviews for you, even if you're not qualified or if the position isn't what you're looking for. Their goal is simple: They want to place you and collect their fee.

- **Don't sign contracts.** Nothing is ever certain. If you don't like the job after you start, you could end up reimbursing the company for the fees it paid the agency. If, however, you feel it is in your best interest to sign a contract, make sure that you understand the meaning of all the clauses first.

- **Accept the job you want.** Don't let the agency pressure you into taking something you have doubts about.

- **Accept only fee-paid jobs.** There are enough companies out there that are willing to pay agency fees. If you accept this financial responsibility, you might have to pay the agency a percentage of your first year's salary. In any case, never pay a penny until you a get a firm job offer. Reputable agencies never charge fees up front.

Job Fairs

Always check the employment section of your local newspaper for announcements of job fairs, which are generally held in convention centers or large hotels. (The ads will usually list the names of companies that will be there.) These fairs are great opportunities to meet representatives from dozens of companies who have gathered for the sole purpose of looking for new employees. Do as much research as you can. When you go, take a clean stack of resumes and dress in conservative business clothes.

Temporary Agencies

These organizations are no longer just sources of clerical and office help. Today they comprise a multibillion-dollar industry that provides temps in all professions—from computer programming to nursing. Most people don't think of companies that specialize in temporary help as sources of permanent income, but they should. At the very least, accepting a temporary assignment can be an excellent way to showcase your talents. Odds are that if the company has a need and likes what it sees, you will eventually be offered a permanent position. At the very least, temp work can be a safety net until you find the job you want.

YOUR PLAN OF ACTION

A plan set into motion will yield results. Get organized and then push yourself to be the best you can.

- Write a resume that packages your qualifications into an effective advertisement.
- Activate and improve your network. Don't fail to tap into all sources of potential employers.
- Review the classified employment advertisements in the newspaper. If you find an ad that interests you, research the company and then, if you like what you see, send a resume.

- Research a minimum of five potential employers per week and send resumes.
- Call at least five networking contacts per week; follow up by sending thank-you letters and, if appropriate, resumes.
- Expand your network by gaining one new contact per day.

Chapter 4

WINNING RESUMES

An effective resume can be a powerful tool in getting you the job you want. But it's more than that: It's another way to identify what you like to do and clarify what you could do in the future.

Many minorities, especially those with minimal or no job experience, have a hard time writing a resume because they tend to take their skills for granted and think they have little to show for themselves. To overcome this, you need to think of what you have done in different terms.

For example, if you're a recent graduate, have you helped organize or lead university or community groups? Have you done volunteer or part-time work or internships? You can break down all these activities into specific skills. If you've already started your career—regardless of your field—have you been involved with training, administration, management, budget development, or planning for your company? Have you written technical papers, developed briefing materials, or made oral presentations? Have you motivated others to achieve work-related goals? These are skills. You need to unearth them and put them down on paper. Don't dwell on the skills you *don't* have.

RESUME BASICS

Experts often debate such details as resume format and length. But they all agree on one thing: A resume is not your life story.

Resumes should be crisp, brief, and to the point. This is where identifying your skills comes in handy. The reader wants meat, not gravy. Remember, the object is to get an interview. The interview, not the resume, is what leads to a job offer. But the resume is what gets your foot in the door.

> **The interview is what leads to the job offer. But the resume is what gets your foot in the door.**

All resumes create a unique portrait; there's no cookie-cutter version that fits all job seekers. Most employers do, however, have strong preferences when it comes to style and content.

It can take up to six minutes to read a couple of single-spaced pages. Managers don't have the time, especially when they might be dealing with dozens, or hundreds, of resumes. When a batch of resumes arrives on their desk, they don't read them; they scan. You won't survive the scan if you use large, dense blocks of words. Readers want, reasonably enough, readability. That is, wide margins; bold headings; bullets; tight, compact paragraphs; and pointed objectives or qualification summaries. They also want brevity: Keep resumes to one to two pages.

THE CUSTOM RESUME

Develop a master resume, then tailor variations to respond to specific openings. The master resume should list all your work experiences in chronological order, including companies, titles, dates, specific accomplishments, and skills.

Your goal is to develop a marketing brochure for yourself. The format you select will depend on your level of experience. For example, if you are a recent college graduate, you should probably lead off with an objective. If, however, you have more than four years' experience, you might decide to start with an experience summary.

Next, decide how the resume should be organized. The basic approaches are chronological and functional. If you are ever in doubt about which approach to choose, the chronological format is usually preferred.

Chronological

In this format work history is organized chronologically, with the most recent information listed first. Job titles and organizations are emphasized. This approach is easy to read and can be used to emphasize professional growth. It is best suited to job seekers whose objectives are closely aligned with their work history.

It's advantageous when:
- you recently graduated and are just starting your career
- recent employers or job titles are impressive
- your career path shows steady advancement
- you are planning to stay in the same field

It's not advantageous when:
- you have a history of frequent job changes
- you want to change fields or careers
- you have gaps in your employment history

Functional

Functional resumes are organized under functional skill headings rather than by year. Employment history is secondary to your demonstrable skills and is usually briefly stated at the close of the resume.

It's advantageous when:

- you are changing careers
- you want to emphasize skills you haven't used recently
- you want to focus on abilities rather than job history
- you have a variety of unrelated work experience or you have been working temporary assignments

It's not advantageous when:

- you want to emphasize strong career growth
- you have a history in highly traditional fields such as accounting or education
- you have little work experience

Start at the Beginning

Focus on your achievements and the employer's hiring needs. Don't include personal information (age, marital status, ethnic origin, hobbies) or a photo. Employers may use these to screen out minority candidates.

There are three to five basic parts to most resumes: (1) your career objective (optional), (2) an experience summary (optional), (3) experience, (4) special skills or honors, and (5) education. How you format your resume will depend on your career level.

RESUMES FOR RECENT GRADUATES

- Begin with your name in capitals and boldface type.
- Include your complete address and zip code.
- Always include day and evening telephone numbers.
- List your degree(s). Include your grade point average only if it is impressive.
- List relevant reports, papers, research assignments.
- Include extracurricular or volunteer activities that show responsibility and achievement.
- List part-time or summer jobs and internships.
- If you are willing to travel or relocate, say so.
- List special skills such as foreign language proficiency or computer knowledge. But don't list skills that obviously aren't applicable to the position you seek.
- You may conclude your resume with "References available upon request." (But it's not necessary.)

RESUMES FOR EXPERIENCED PROFESSIONALS

Chronological

- Begin with your current or most recent position and work backwards chronologically. Recent experience should be more detailed than past jobs.
- If your job titles relate to your stated objective, start each position description with them. If not, begin with the company's name.

Functional

- Develop functional skill headings.
- Describe your skills and expertise in one-line phrases and place them under the appropriate headings.
- Go back and rank your phrases and place them in order—starting with the most important one first.
- Bake sure you don't exceed one page for this type of resume.

Writing Tips

Fuzzy objectives or qualification summaries are apt to make the reader toss your resume into the also-ran pile. Here's an unfortunate but common example:

Objective: Challenging and responsible position in which I can make a meaningful....

First of all, do you know anyone who wants a boring or irresponsible job? Probably not. How about this:

Objective: Product Sales Support

Better, but the reader still doesn't know what role you want to play. Be more specific. If the reader can't tell what you want, he or she can only assume you don't know either. But be careful if you decide to use an objective. Too broad is bad, but being *too* specific can eliminate you from consideration for other openings the company might have.

Experience or qualification summaries up front in a resume can be effective attention-grabbers. But you have to be both brief and specific. If, for example, you say "software engineering," you need to specify language and operating systems. Or if you list "financial analysis," you need to indicate the environment: Wall Street? A bank? A department store?

Describe your skills in concise, clear terms. Back them up by referring to concrete experiences and accomplishments. For example, if you designed a new program that saved your company money or time, say:

"Directed the design of a new automated system that improved data-entry productivity 40 percent."

Don't say:

"Responsible for improving productivity."

Always try to make a clear connection between your skills and the needs of an employer. There is no such thing as unrelated experience.

Consider how Carl turned college business experience into an asset when he applied for a sales position. During his sophomore year, he invested in 20 pairs of roller skates. On weekends he rented them out by the hour to students. On his resume

> **Make a clear connection between your skills and an employer's needs. There is no such thing as unrelated experience.**

he didn't say, "Operated a skate-rental business." Instead, he linked his experience to sales by saying, "Founded and operated profitable part-time skate-rental business. Handled all marketing and promotional efforts and management, which yielded a 90 percent use rate...."

Resume readers expect you to brag, but don't overdo it. Let your achievements and titles speak for themselves. Terms like *aggressive*, *dynamic*, and *powerful* can't be measured. But don't be a wimp, either. For instance, terms like *assisted*, *aided*, and *helped to achieve* make you sound like a person with little or no responsibility.

Always strive for clarity and specificity. Ask yourself: What *action verbs* describe tasks? What is the *object* of the action? What was the *outcome* of the effort?

Some more tips:

- **Don't use personal pronouns.** For example, don't say, "I looked up data for a report." Avoid "I" and say, "Researched over 20 labor studies for a report...."
- **Use as many verbs as practical.** Make sure you use the active, not the passive, voice. For example, don't say, "The design for xx was created by me...." Instead try, "I designed the...."
- **Use short sentences.** Don't ramble.
- **Avoid jargon or uncommon abbreviations** unless they are standard to your field.
- **Define your achievements in concrete terms.** For example, don't say, "I improved quality." Instead try, "Reduced defects over 50 percent...."
- **Edit. Reedit. Then edit again.** Nothing creates a worse impression than typos or grammatical errors on your resume.
- **Avoid bright, fancy paper.** Use high-quality white (or off-white) bond paper. If you decide you don't want the expense of having your resume printed, a clean, crisp photocopy is acceptable. (Letters, though, must always be originals.) If you are using a personal computer and word

processing package and you have a laser or high-quality dot-matrix printer, print a stack of originals.

Common Resume Mistakes

Make sure your resume isn't:

- too long or overloaded with heavy blocks of text. Be concise.
- too brief; lacking meaningful information
- poorly formatted and typed, hard to read, disorganized, or unattractive
- not results-oriented; lacking concrete accomplishments
- too fluffy or filled with irrelevant facts
- marred by misspelled words, typos, or poor grammar
- unprofessional. Elaborate typesetting, binders, photographs, and exotic paper are the marks of an amateur.
- poorly focused. Employers need to know what you want and what you can do. Your skills should match their needs.
- misdirected. Too many resumes are sent to the wrong office or person. Cover letters help prevent this.

ATTENTION-GRABBING COVER LETTERS

Your letter shouldn't be merely a cover sheet for your resume. It's the first impression an employer is going to have of you, so write it with care.

A cover letter should be brief, friendly, enthusiastic, and informative. But remember to keep the tone professional; don't try to be overly familiar or chummy with the reader.

Start Right

Avoid beginning with "Dear Sir/Madam." Pick up the telephone and make an effort to find out the right person's name. From there, you can start your letter in one of several ways.

Researched starts are based on your legwork. Begin by mentioning something you learned when researching the company or from a story written about the organization. For example, "Since you have acquired the ABC company, I believe you might be interested in my marketing achievements for their X product line." Or you might open with "I enjoyed reading the interview with you that was published in the Z Magazine. Because of my experience with ABC products, you might find the following interesting...."

A **referenced introduction** tells the reader you have been recommended by someone. For instance: "Mr. Jones of the XYZ company has suggested you might be interested in my expertise as a marketing representative." One note of caution, though: Make sure your reference is known and respected by the person you are writing to.

Accomplishment can be a powerful attention-grabber, if used properly. "During my first six months as head of marketing for the ABC company, sales increased over 75 percent." Don't write "I am applying for the recently advertised marketing director position because I think I'm qualified."

Consider the experience of Vicki, a computer scientist who specialized in documentation. For almost two months she sent out resumes in response to openings for technical writers. She typically started her cover letter like this:

In response to your advertisement for position X, I have enclosed a copy of my resume. Since I was responsible for the development of user documentation at the ABC Company, I believe you might find my background interesting.

Finally, on the advice of a friend, she changed her lead to:

I am delighted to have this opportunity to respond to your announcement for a lead software documentation writer. As you will see in the enclosed resume, I recently wrote the complete ABC user manual. This 500-page book has already become the standard guide for clients using the system...."

Within two weeks, Vicki had accepted a position with a software engineering company.

A winning resume will result in invitations to meet with potential employers. Now you must sell your skills in person as effectively as you have done on paper.

Recent Graduate

David Garcia
1111 California Street
Los Angeles, CA 00000
213/555-1234 (H)

OBJECTIVE:
Entry-level management position in a retail environment.

EDUCATION:
Bachelor of Science, business administration, University of Arizona, June 1993. Maintained a 3.5 GPA last six semesters.

EXPERIENCE:
Smith Stores, Tucson, AZ. Worked part time, averaging 15 hours a week, from July 1991 to June 1993.

- Customer Service Department. Wrote letters in response to customer inquiries. Manned the customer service desk hot line and answered appliance warranty questions.

- Wrote advertising copy and developed layouts.

- Indoor Sales Department. Sold merchandise in a variety of departments. Consistently exceeded sales quotas. Was named part-time salesperson of the month seven times.

- Office administration. Assisted with bookkeeping and inventory control. Developed new automated inventory control system that reduced out-of-stock time by 50 percent.

ACTIVITIES:
- Fundraising chairperson for 1992 drive to expand the local high school computer laboratory. Organized effort, wrote letters, and solicited help of local business establishments. Raised over $50,000.

- Tutored high school students in English and writing.

References provided upon request.

Chronological with Objective

Robert Johnson
1111 Maryland Street
Baltimore, MD 00000
410/555-1234 (H)
410/444-1234 (W)

OBJECTIVE:
Management position in corporate finance or accounting organization.

EXPERIENCE:

XYZ Corporation (1986–Present), Senior Finance Officer for retail operations. Direct the development and cost controls for annual $300 million corporate operating budget.

Established the corporation's first local financial management information system network, which resulted in a 25 percent increase in staff productivity.

Created a corporate training program to familiarize staff with internal audit and budget process.

Saved the corporation $200,000 (over a three-year period) by eliminating the need to contract with outside trainers and consultants.

EFG, Inc. (1984–1986), Internal Auditor for the company accounting department.

Conducted all internal company audits. Reduced external audit hours by 15 percent by developing and implementing a comprehensive audit program.

Established and published standard audit procedures. Conducted in-house audit training for staff members.

ABC Company (1983–1984), Financial Analyst.

Performed financial analyses for the director of budget and finance, including cost analysis, estimating, and computer modeling for new product manufacturing processes.

EDUCATION:
M.B.A., accounting, University of Maryland, 1988
B.S., computer science, American University, 1983

Chronological with Experience Summary

Christine Lee
1111 Manhattan Street
New York, NY 00000
212/555-1234 (H)
212/444-1234 (W)

SUMMARY OF QUALIFICATIONS:

- Ten years experience in accounting and financial execution and planning in manufacturing environments.
- Six years experience designing and implementing automated financial management information systems.
- Four years experience developing corporate financial training programs, including classroom instruction and curriculum development.

EXPERIENCE:

International Computer (1987–present), Financial Operations Officer for manufacturing group. Supervise a staff of 12 accountants and financial analysts. Schedule, monitor, and review budget development and execution.

Reduced accounting department labor costs by $65,000 annually by implementing an automated system. Staff productivity increased over 10 percent.

Developed new monthly financial status report to provide management with "at-a-glance" summaries for key manufacturing indicators and costs.

ABC Company (1983–1987), Senior Financial Analyst. Performed cost estimating and analysis for manufacturing operations. Served as a lead instructor for company automated financial systems training programs.

EDUCATION:

M.B.A., accounting, Columbia University, New York City, 1987
B.S., computer science, Pennsylvania State University, 1983

Functional

Sandra Swanson
1111 Michigan Avenue
Detroit, MI 00000
313/555-1234 (H)

OBJECTIVE:
Manager of technical publications group in an electronic manufacturing environment.

SUMMARY OF QUALIFICATIONS:
- Over eight years experience in electronic systems and equipment development—documenting test, repair, and operating procedures.
- Writing, publishing, and editing—technical manuals and papers, proposals, user guides.

EXPERIENCE:
DEVELOPMENT
- Documented assembly, test, and repair procedures for prototype radar systems.
- Developed and prepared test plans and procedures for prototype navigation satellite systems.

WRITING, EDITING, AND PUBLISHING
- Lead writer for computer repair and user manuals.
- Chief editor and quality-control specialist for a series of computer system manuals.

EMPLOYMENT HISTORY:
ABC Manufacturing, 1988–present
XYZ Laboratories, 1986–1988
EFG Systems, 1985–1986

EDUCATION AND SKILLS:
B.A., English, University of Michigan, 1985
- Selected course work: 30 hours electrical engineering
- Proficient in the use of WordPerfect, Microsoft Word, Freelance, Harvard Graphics, and other software.

Cover Letter

Street Address
City, State, Zip
Telephone No.

Date of Writing

Name
Title
Company
Street Address
City, State, Zip

Dear Ms. X:

I am responding to your recent advertisement in the *Sunday Gazette* for a marketing director. As a senior marketing representative for the ABC company, I increased sales over 50 percent in two years.

The enclosed resume summarizes my experience in marketing computer supplies. The marketing initiatives I developed during last year's industry realignment might be of particular interest to you. Since your corporation recently acquired the XYZ Company and is expanding into the medium-sized business market, I believe I could apply my skills to this new venture.

I would like to discuss this vacancy with you and will call next Monday morning to set up a meeting at your convenience. In the meantime, please contact me if I can provide additional information about my qualifications.

Sincerely,

Your Signature
Your typed name
Enclosure: As stated

Chapter 5

INTERVIEWING AND THE JOB OFFER

If you have presented yourself effectively on paper and opened the door, it's time to present yourself well in person. That's the winning combination. Yet an unbelievable number of applicants fail at this point in the hiring process. Don't be one of them.

For minorities the interview is the most dangerous phase of the job search because the odds are good that any prejudice the interviewer might have will manifest itself now. But by demonstrating poise, skill, likability, and professionalism, you can stack the odds in your favor and succeed. Along the way, you just might explode some myths and negative stereotypes.

WINNING WAYS

Interviewing etiquette demands certain basic behavior. Without it, even though you may be a genius who could contribute immeasurably to the company's success, you probably won't get the job.

- **Don't go unprepared.** If you do, the worst moment of your interview will come when you're asked "What do you know or like about our company?" Also, research can help you avoid an interview for a job you aren't interested in or qualified to perform.

- **Go well-rested.** It could be a long day, especially at large companies.
- **Be on time—or early.** But don't be more than five minutes early, or you may annoy a busy interviewer who's on a tight schedule.
- **Always treat secretaries and receptionists with respect.** Not only because it's the right thing to do, but because a surprising number of managers will ask them what they thought of you.
- **Look good.** There's no way to overstate the importance of appearance in corporate America. Like it or not, you will be judged according to long-established standards for business attire. Men should generally wear a darkish suit (navy and charcoal gray are good choices) with a muted tie and well-polished shoes. Women have a bit more leeway; a suit or a tailored dress, with low-key jewelry and makeup, are best for more conservative firms.
- **Have the right information.** Bring an extra copy of your resume, along with a list of references (complete with addresses and phone numbers), letters of recommendation, and all other pertinent information.
- **Smile and show enthusiasm.** Nothing disarms a skeptic or someone who's not used to dealing one-on-one with minorities more than this.
- **Always thank people for their time and interest when your interview is finished.** Follow up with a written thank-you note and restate your interest.

Overlook any of these elements at your peril. Here's what happened to Kim. When she was called in for an interview with a midsized manufacturing firm in Cincinnati, she was ecstatic.

She had done some research on the company, but she quickly rushed out to the library to dig deeper.

Kim arrived early for the interview, filled out an application form, and was told that she would be talking to the manager and two senior technical staff members. She was pleasantly surprised when the second person she talked to turned out to be Asian American also.

She thought that the interviews went well, and the interviewers promised to get back to her soon. On her way out she was asked to stop by the personnel department because she hadn't completed the reference section of her application. She told personnel she didn't have the addresses and telephone numbers with her but that she would phone in the information as soon as she got home. But she forgot all about it until three days later.

In the meantime, the company decided that Kim was among four candidates who could fill the job. Personnel checked references for the other candidates, and the company made an offer to another candidate before Kim ever got back to them with her information.

> **How the company sees you, the professional, is only half of the hiring equation. The other part is how it sees you, the person.**

She received a form rejection letter. The reason? She had failed to deliver something important. The manager who made the hiring decision felt that either Kim was hiding something and couldn't produce three references or that she wasn't interested enough in the job to follow through.

CREATE THE RIGHT CHEMISTRY

It's essential to sell your skills and assets to interviewers. But having the right qualifications will not always get you a job. You also need to show interest and generate the right chemistry.

How the company sees you, the professional, is only half of the hiring equation. The other part is how it sees you, the person. Of course, this a subjective judgment, but it's an important one nevertheless. You may encounter interviewers who are skeptical or biased against minorities in general, but don't give them reasons not to like you personally.

When you step into the interviewer's corporate world, you need to project professionalism, likability, and enthusiasm. It starts with a firm handshake, a smile, and good eye contact. You should be happy to meet this person—and show it.

Even though you're nervous, speak up. Don't mumble. Remember, the interviewer may be nervous also. You share the burden of avoiding an awkward situation. If the opportunity presents itself, make some interesting small talk.

The interviewer might be having a bad or hectic day and may not feel like taking the time to interview you. Empathize and remember: It's your job to make the interview worthwhile. And don't forget to tell the interviewer that you appreciate his or her time.

As a minority, your ability to project likability could be one of your biggest assets. Use it—and never underestimate the power of people chemistry. (Chapter 6 takes a closer look at the likability factor and how to develop it.)

When John, an African American, interviewed for an administrative job with a Pittsburgh-based communications company, he had no way of knowing that one of his interviewers was going to be a gruff, strongly biased man named Bernie. Among his peer group and friends, Bernie was known as a man who felt that minorities, especially African Americans, received special treatment in school and on the job.

Although he botched a couple of questions, John, an extremely likable man, did well enough with the first two interviewers to stay in the running. Then came Bernie. He fired several preliminary questions, and John answered them well. But the older man was clearly not impressed. At that point, John noticed several golf trophies enclosed in a glass bookcase. During a lull in the questioning, John said he was a golfer and asked Bernie if he was one also. Bernie answered yes and studied the young African American with new interest. After several minutes of golf talk, they returned to the business at hand. But the tone of the interview had become more relaxed and friendly.

On the strength of Bernie's evaluation form, John was hired. Given his reputation, Bernie's recommendation caused more than a few raised eyebrows. The bottom line: Look for common ground to build bridges and relationships. You might find new allies and friends among the most unlikely people.

AVOIDING A BAD INTERVIEW

Interviewers range from intimidating to open and friendly. You are going to meet them all, and you need to develop sharp observational skills to analyze and cope with their various styles.

Never lose your cool or get rattled. For instance, the interviewer might study your resume and application and then unexpectedly say, "Your grades were average. Did you like school?"

Think before speaking, and try to field the question smoothly. Perhaps you worked your way through school, and it cut into study time. Say so. Maybe you had a heavy credit load. Tell the interviewer that you wanted to finish school as quickly as possible because you were eager to enter the work force. Did you perform better in laboratories than in classrooms? Explain that you like the practical better than the theoretical. Such answers tend to neutralize tough questions.

Another popular interview tactic is for the interviewer to lapse into long periods of silence, perhaps to see how you will react. Don't become jumpy or squirm in your chair, and don't start rambling. But if the silence lasts too long, break it. Ask a question about the organization or new projects. This will put the ball in the interviewer's court.

Some interviewers can only be described as offbeat or downright odd. Julie, a young Japanese-American professional, recalls interviewing with a large computer-supply company for an outside sales position: "I knew I was in trouble when the interviewer leaned back in her chair and closed her eyes for several minutes. Suddenly she sat up straight, grabbed a pad of paper off her desk, dropped it, and barked, 'I'm a buyer. Sell me this paper.'"

Julie admits, "At first I just sat there startled, with my mouth half open." But then she realized this was a great opportunity, and she plunged ahead. "I took a deep breath and went on to describe how the paper was indispensable to her office needs. I told her it was exceptionally high quality, and that if she would buy it by the box, I could give her a great price. She smiled, and I knew I was in." In other words, she played the interviewer's little game and won the job.

Another favorite ploy of interviewers, especially with minorities, is to start talking about things that are unrelated to the job. For example, the interviewer says, "So you are from Mexico. I've always wondered what it would be like to live there."

Try to combine his interest in your native country with the job opening. Perhaps you might say something like, "Growing up there was wonderful because of the cultural richness and the natural beauty of the country. Technology, though, has had the same impact there as it has in other places. For example, my small city was never the same after the ABC Company built an assembly plant there. Suddenly there was a large influx of technicians and engineers living there. In fact, that's where I first developed an interest in manufacturing automation...." This way you can successfully steer the conversation back to the business at hand.

Likability could be one of your biggest assets. Use it—and never underestimate the power of people chemistry.

Be prepared for anything and know how to cope with different personalities. Here are some examples:

■ **Arrogant**—Get such interviewers talking by asking questions about their career. Express your respect for what they have accomplished. Link it to your goals by describing how your interests overlap.

- **Shy or uninterested**—Try to hit them with your best shot right up front. For instance, "My marketing team was able to increase sales over 40 percent when we...." Also, try to find common ground to get them to open up. For example, "I noticed that you are responsible for redesigning all of the corporate marketing material. That's something I've always been interested in. I believe that is the key to effective...."

- **Nervous or stressed out**—Let them know that you appreciate their valuable time. Help them out. For instance, "I know this is a hectic time of the year for your department, so why don't I just give you a brief overview of how my experience might fit into your activities?"

- **Disorganized**—Keep interviews on track by logically explaining how your qualifications fit the interviewers' needs.

- **Formal or rigid**—Stick to the facts. No jokes or quips. Always use "Mr." or "Ms." Never slouch; sit tall.

THE MOST FREQUENTLY ASKED QUESTIONS

If you listen, good interviewers will either hint at or tell you what they are looking for in an employee when they talk about the company. When they get down to the business at hand, most interviewers ask questions along similar lines. These generally relate to how your skills, knowledge, and work experience fit with their needs. Listen and respond accordingly. You can expect any combination of these questions. If you're prepared with good answers, you're ready to face anyone and win. Remember, questions are opportunities to deliver selling points.

1. What do you know about our company?

STRATEGY: In addition to spouting off the normal "I know you make gizmos and had sales last year of $50 million," try to demonstrate that you've done your homework and have a deeper understanding. For example, "I believe your merger with the ABC Company last year and the introduction of your supergizmo have positioned the company to dominate the gizmo market." This a question that a surprising number of interviewees stumble over.

2. Why did you decide to seek a position with our company?

STRATEGY: In addition to saying that you like the business or feel that it provides great opportunities, try to be specific. For example, "I want to work on the leading edge of gizmo technology, and I believe your company provides this opportunity."

3. Tell me about yourself and your background.

STRATEGY: By this time, interviewers should have already dropped some strong hints about what they are looking for. Don't just recite the facts on your resume. Try to relate your experience to what they want from the person they hire.

4. What are you looking for in a position?

STRATEGY: Outline what you want, and describe why you feel the company can provide the opportunity and environment to achieve it. Emphasize how this match could benefit the company.

5. Your resume says you did (whatever). Could you tell me more about that?

STRATEGY: Be intimately familiar with your resume, and be prepared to explain any part of it.

6. Do you have plans for continued study?

STRATEGY: It's usually good to show interest in professional growth—whether through pursuing an advanced degree or going to night school to stay current on the latest in your field.

7. What subject did you like best in school? Or: "Describe your most rewarding college experience."

STRATEGY: Relate your achievements to the job requirements.

8. What are your career goals and objectives?

STRATEGY: Try to show that you are well focused and you know what you want. If you did your homework in Chapter 2, this should be easy. Keep it focused, though, within the context of the company. For example, don't say, "I would really like to start my own gizmo company." If your goal is to eventually get into management, say so. If it is to perform research, say that.

9. What do you see yourself doing in five years?

STRATEGY: Relate this to your goals, but be careful. For example, don't say, "I would like to have your job as manager of gizmo design and production."

10. What do you consider to be your greatest strength? Weakness?

STRATEGY: Focus on either technical or management strengths. Try not to dwell on weaknesses. For example, you might say, "I don't have a great deal of experience, but I certainly have the training and people skills to do the job."

11. In what ways do you think you can make a contribution to our operation?

STRATEGY: You should know enough about what the company does so you can show how your experience and skills fit.

12. **What salary do you want?**

STRATEGY: This is dangerous ground. And many interviewees blow the interview at this point. You don't want to underprice yourself, but you also don't want to price yourself out of a job. Don't say, "I need a salary of about XX dollars." Or "I won't settle for less than XX dollars." Instead say, "I would prefer that you make an offer." Or "What is the standard pay scale for a junior gizmo designer?" Or "I'm really interested in long-term growth and advancement, and my salary requirements are negotiable." Or "I'm interested in a career with your company, not a job. I'm willing to consider whatever your company pays junior gizmo designers." The secret is to get them talking so you can find out what salary they have in mind.

13. **Are you willing to travel?**

STRATEGY: This may not matter. If, however, you know that travel is required in the job, try to get more details. For example, "I am accustomed (or willing) to travel up to xx days per month. Does the position call for more travel than that?"

14. **When can you start?**

STRATEGY: If you don't have any commitments or current job, you can say immediately, or next Monday, or whatever seems reasonable. If, however, you are employed, always say, "I would like to give xx weeks' notice to give my boss a chance to find a suitable replacement." Two weeks is the minimum; anything less shows a lack of consideration and professionalism. And if you don't give your current employer notice, new employers will suspect that you'll do the same thing to them.

The following additional questions apply only to those who

are already into their careers and interviewing for a new position:

1. **Why do you want to change jobs?** Or: Why did you leave your last job?

STRATEGY: If you were laid off, say so. There is no stigma attached to being cut from a company in our turbulent economic times. The standard answer, though, for someone seeking a better job is "I want more challenges and greater rewards." Or "I have skills that aren't being used." You might, however, want to be more specific. For example, "When I was hired, it was my understanding that I would have my own gizmo division within two years. Due to reorganization, though, that possibility now seems remote. Therefore, after a lot of soul-searching, I've decided to look elsewhere."

2. **What did you like best about your last (or present) job?**

STRATEGY: Be honest, but be careful here. If you say, "I enjoyed the challenge of designing a hand-held gizmo," be prepared to then answer the following question: "So why do you want to leave such a challenging job?"

3. **How did (or didn't) you get along with your boss?**

STRATEGY: Never criticize your boss, even if you think he or she is an arrogant jerk. Be diplomatic. For example, "Mr. Jones was very involved in the daily activities related to gizmo design, so our product received top management attention. I was the chief gizmo designer, and I believe we had an effective working relationship. I respected his ability."

4. **What major problem have you encountered on the job and how did you solve it?**

STRATEGY: This could be any type of management or technical problem. For example, "When we were trying to miniaturize the gizmo, we were limited by the current materials available. I reorganized our division to include a materials research group. As a result, we were able to develop the alloy needed to achieve our gizmo size goal." Be careful here. You are usually on safer ground describing a technical problem than a people problem.

5. What do you feel was your greatest achievement on the job?

STRATEGY: Be specific. For example, "As I've mentioned, I think being able to design the supergizmo and bring it into production under cost projections was a significant achievement."

In the end, all interviews boil down to basics. Most employers won't be satisfied unless you can answer the two bottom-line questions: "Are you qualified to do the job?" and "Will you fit into our corporate culture?"

ILLEGAL QUESTIONS AND HOW TO HANDLE THEM

Some interviewers are not aware that they are asking illegal questions during interviews. Those who are aware usually want to address a legitimate concern, but others may have personal reasons for trying to trip you up, intimidate you, or make you feel you don't qualify for the job.

All job candidates should have an interest in illegal questions, especially if they mask hidden agendas. As a minority, you should have an even stronger interest.

When asked an illegal or improper question during an interview, you have a couple of choices. You can refuse to respond, period. Or you can respond with tact so that you don't alienate those who are trying to address a real concern. This second approach sends a signal to those who might have a hidden agenda that you are wise to their ways and they might do well to back off. Unless you are extremely sensitive, this is the best way to handle such questions.

Don't lie, but try to neutralize improper questions. Never lose your cool. Be on the alert for questions that smack of racism. These tend to be questions that are clearly not job-related.

Commonly Asked Illegal Questions

1. **Exactly what race are you?**

STRATEGY: Try to neutralize the question. Say, "I'm not sure how that relates to this job. Can you explain?" If interviewers can't come up with a logical or plausible explanation, they will probably move on.

2. **How did you get to this country?**

STRATEGY: You need to decide whether this question is a put-down or a show of genuine interest. For instance, something you said may have lead interviewers to believe you are from a Communist country such as China or Cuba, and they are interested. This can be an opportunity to show how persistent and resourceful you are. If it bothers you, though, you can always express confusion about how this relates to the job.

3. **You graduated from XX University. How did you get into that school? Were you admitted under the affirmative action program?**

STRATEGY: If you feel it's none of their business, you can be vague. You might say, "It's a great school. I met all the entrance requirements and satisfied all the course requirements to earn my XX degree."

4. **What do your parents do?**

STRATEGY: This may or may not be innocent. For example, the interviewer is trying to find out whether you have the ability to bring business into the firm through family contacts. In any case, you might say something like, "My parents are retired." Or "My mother works for the government." This doesn't reveal what she does if you don't want to discuss it.

5. **What was your original or maiden name?**

STRATEGY: Interviewers usually ask this of Hispanic or Asian Americans. The reason? They may be trying to pin you down about where you are from. Or they might just be curious. For example, suppose you are from Thailand and look Oriental, and your name is Fred Smith. Unless your English is perfect and you appear to be a first- or second-generation American, they know you probably weren't born with that name. You might say, "My original name was hard to pronounce for most Americans, so I had it changed." Or, if the question bothers you, try politely saying something like "Can you tell me how that's pertinent to this discussion?"

6. **Are you married? Do you have children? Do you plan on getting married and starting a family? Who's going to take care of your children while you work?**

STRATEGY: These are all related questions. If you don't want to indicate your status, politely say, "I didn't realize a person's marital status was a consideration for this job." The question of childcare can be handled by saying something like "I assume what you are really asking is whether absenteeism or punctuality will be a problem. I can assure you it won't be. My previous employment proves this." Or if you don't have kids, you might say, "I plan to pursue a career regardless of whether I decide to start a family."

7. **Is your spouse employed?**

STRATEGY: Some organizations believe that if your spouse is employed, you will be less motivated to work hard. Neutralize the question. For example, you might say, "Yes, and he or she is very supportive of my career (or my seeking employment)."

8. **Do you own a home or rent?**

STRATEGY: Again, this may be small talk, but it's an invasion of your privacy and status away from the office. Unless you are willing to discuss it, say, "I'm not sure how that relates to this job. Can you tell me?"

9. **Have you ever sued anyone?**

STRATEGY: They are plainly trying to find out if you are what they consider a "troublemaker." They may be specifically trying to find out if you have ever complained of discrimination and taken any type of legal action. This is a definite red flag about the company. If you have or if you are in the process of doing so, the best thing is to be honest.

10. **How old are you?**

STRATEGY: Unless you want to answer, just smile and say, "I believe I'm old enough to have developed the skills required to do this job."

11. **What church do you attend?**

STRATEGY: Ask how the question is relevant to the position. Or be vague: "I attend a local church."

12. **Have you ever been arrested?**

STRATEGY: If you haven't, a simple "no" will suffice. If you have, smile and say, "I've never done anything that would give your corporation any concern about trust or honesty." Then, if you have good personal and professional references, you might add, "I believe my personal integrity is reflected in my references." Laws regarding this question vary from state to state. In general, it is legal to ask only about convictions, not arrests. But there are exceptions. For example, suppose you are applying for a job with a company that requires Department of Defense or national security clearances. In this case you should be forthcoming. Or if you are a candidate for a bank teller position, the company may deny you the job on the basis of a previous conviction for theft.

13. **Are you a citizen?**

STRATEGY: You may be required to prove citizenship after accepting a job. For an interview, though, you should only be asked if you are authorized to work in the U.S.

14. **How is your credit rating?**

STRATEGY: This probably has nothing to do with the job, but don't lie. It's easy for the company to run a credit check on you. Some employers routinely do that to see if a candidate is responsible and in good standing. It's not a matter of the size of your credit line so much as whether you have fulfilled your financial obligations. If your rating is fine, say so. If you have had some problems—short of major financial disasters—try something like "I assume you are asking if I have ever filed bankruptcy or defaulted on a loan. The answer is no."

15. **How did you learn a foreign language?**

STRATEGY: Interviewers can't legally ask how you learned any foreign language or whether a particular foreign language is your native tongue. They can, however, ask what languages you speak fluently. Usually answering this is a plus because of the increasing emphasis on international business and cultural diversity in the workplace.

WHY YOU DIDN'T GET THE JOB

You may have thought that you didn't do too well during the interview, so when the rejection letter came, you weren't surprised. Or maybe you thought you did great, so it came as something of a shock. But even well-qualified candidates commonly make mistakes that can undermine a good fit.

There are eleven common reasons why interviewees don't land the job. *Remember, the odds favor you because nine of these goofs are under your control.* (Only numbers 10 and 11 are not.) Some of the "big 11" may be related, but they are all separate issues.

1. **Being poorly prepared.**

2. **Arriving late for the interview.**

3. **Dressing inappropriately.**

4. **Lacking enthusiasm and likability.**

5. **Making negative remarks about former employers or co-workers.**

6. **Being arrogant, overconfident, or a know-it-all.** You can promote yourself and your strengths without coming across as abrasive.

7. **Failing to ask questions about the company and its activities or asking the wrong questions.** Interviewers usually like to talk about the company in response to questions about such things as products or plans for expansion. However, asking "What are the hours?" is a mistake that ranks right up there with "How much money will I make?" It gives the impression that you're a clock-watcher. Let the interviewer bring up the subject of normal work hours.

8. **Responding poorly to questions.** If you answer "yes" or "no" to most questions, you are not promoting dialogue or dis-

cussion that can link your skills to the company's needs. Also, if you lead questions in the direction of "What can the company do for me," you are making a mistake. Sell yourself and how you can contribute to the company's needs.

9. **Asking about salary.** Let the interviewer bring up this subject.

10. **Losing out to someone better qualified.**

11. **Not fitting the company's culture.** This can be an excuse for not hiring minorities, and since it's very subjective, it's tough to fight. If, however, you demonstrate your professionalism and strive to create the right chemistry, you can reduce the odds of being turned down.

LANDING THE JOB

If the company does want you, you need to decide if you feel the same way. The factors to consider fall into four major categories, and you should carefully consider each:

1. The position
2. Your potential boss
3. The company
4. The offer

THE POSITION

It's always wise to try to answer the following questions:

- **Have they clearly spelled out your responsibilities?** (And are these responsibilities and demands compatible with your lifestyle? For instance, if you are expected to work nights and weekends, will that interfere with your plans to go to school or your family responsibilities?)

- **Do the performance goals set for the position seem realistic and attainable?**
- **How long have they been trying to fill the vacancy?**
- **What happened to the previous incumbent?** (Did he or she quit? Get fired? Promoted? After how long in the job?)
- **What is the growth potential?** (Do you have room to go up? Is there any mobility to transfer around within the organization?)
- **How are salary increases determined?** (Are they based purely on performance or are cost-of-living increases part of the equation? How often will you be considered for pay increases?)
- **Does the company expect more than 40 hours a week?** (This is especially crucial if you are a salaried employee. Many professionals are expected to work well in excess of a standard 40-hour week even though they are paid a set salary.)

YOUR POTENTIAL BOSS

- **How long has he or she been in the position? At the company?**
- **Does his or her age seem to be consistent with the position?** (This can be a clue about growth potential. For instance, if the boss is too old for a junior management position, you have to wonder if the company offers any opportunity to move up.)

- **To whom does he or she report?** (Generally, the higher up that person is, the better, because it means your boss must have a fair amount of power.)
- **When you interviewed, did there seem to be good chemistry between you and the potential boss?**

THE COMPANY

- **Is it financially sound and stable?**
- **How long has it been in business?**
- **Is it a growing company? Has it been profitable?**
- **What is the health of its industry?**
- **Is it prominent in the industry?**
- **What is its overall reputation?**
- **Does it have a history of layoffs or cutbacks?**
- **Have the people you interviewed with been working there for a reasonable period of time?**
- **Do the corporate personality and environment seem right?** (This goes beyond the physical building. When you interviewed and walked through the facility, did it seem like the type of operation you would be comfortable in?)
- **Is it conveniently located?** (Ask yourself if the daily commute is going to become a grind. Can you take public transportation?)

Lies Companies Tell Prospective New Employees

They may be stated in different terms, but there are seven common lies that companies tell when trying to lure new employees into their ranks. In fairness, the majority of organizations in corporate America won't try to deceive you. During your career, though, some will. Beware if a company does tell you something that you know to be untrue. Of course, it may just be an overly enthusiastic recruiter trying to put the best light on things. But it may be a deliberate lie. The seven top falsehoods:

1. **The company is solid financially.** Remember, just because the company has been around for awhile doesn't mean it is in good shape. On the other hand, the fact that the company lost money last year doesn't mean that it's going out of business. Always look at the overall picture of a company's health.

2. **You'll be your own person and have complete autonomy.** Unless it's an unusually progressive, freewheeling company or you are being hired to run the organization, you'll have to answer to someone. You will seldom find complete independence; so if someone promises it, ask questions.

3. **The sky's the limit. You can go as far as you want.** Sure, but depending on the company, that may not be too far. The other catch is that there are generally written or unwritten time constraints. For instance, higher-ups may say, "You must have two years as a systems analyst before you can be considered for promotion to a senior systems analyst."

4. **I can guarantee that you will be successful here.** No one can guarantee you anything. And they shouldn't give you the impression that they can.

5. **You'll be groomed for top management.** No one has yet seen you in action, so it's unrealistic to promise you this.

6. **We guarantee that we'll train you.** This may sound great, but in reality, you may not be given the opportunity to receive formal training. Later, if you complain, you will be told

that you received valuable on-the-job training (whether or not this was true).

7. **We always promote from within.** This may give prospective employees the illusion that if they work hard they can make it to the executive suite in time. To be sure, some companies do always promote from within or have an aggressive in-house training program. So when they say they can deliver, it's the truth. But many companies' managerial and executive ranks are full of outsiders.

You may not find out the answers to all of your questions. But the more you know, the more informed your decision will be. And the better your odds of success. Ideally, of course, you should talk to someone who works for the company. If you don't know anyone, you will have to rely on your personal observations and homework.

THE OFFER

Everything in your compensation package has a dollar value. Pay is obviously a primary consideration, but you need to consider the total package. From stock options and bonuses to vacation and health care, it's the total that counts.

For example, if company A offers you an annual starting salary of $30,000 and company B offers $28,000, which is the better offer? That depends. Suppose at company A you have to pay for your own health insurance premiums at a cost of $400 per month ($4,800 per year), but company B pays 100 percent. Even though company B pays less, your take-home pay is going to be more.

Analyze all offer factors before signing up. And if you honestly feel you can sweeten the offer through negotiation, go for it. But be extremely careful that the points you raise are well thought out and reasonable.

Getting the Best Deal

Salary negotiations take place at some point after a successful job interview. Usually both sides can agree on an acceptable figure. Yet even though the company may only be willing to pay a certain amount, that doesn't preclude you from taking steps to get a better deal.

For instance, suppose the standard employee performance evaluation is conducted once a year on your employment anniversary. This is generally when you receive a pay raise. You can try to negotiate an agreement for a special review after your first six months, which will send the message that you plan on working hard and succeeding. Or suppose you are on a straight salary (not paid hourly), but you know your boss will expect you to work extra hours during certain peak periods. Try to negotiate time off as compensation.

Always approach such negotiation with confidence, but don't be unreasonably demanding. Be tactful. For instance, if the company only offers new employees two weeks' vacation, you probably won't be able to get three weeks, no matter how hard you push. Plus, asking for concessions the company can't grant or that are out of line with your position can cause a good deal to go sour and get you off on the wrong foot with your new company. Or, in the worst case, the company may even withdraw its offer.

Benefits

- **Vacation**—How much will you get to start? Does it meet your needs? Is it at least up to industry standards? (A minimum of two weeks per year.) What is the maximum amount of paid time off?
- **Holidays**—Does the company offer standard federal government observances?
- **Sick leave**—What is the company policy? Does it accrue so that you can carry it over to the next year?
- **Medical/dental/disability insurance**—Does the company pay? If not, what will it cost you per month? With spiraling health-care costs, this can be a big-ticket item that could cost you thousands of dollars per year.
- **Retirement**—What is the vesting time? As a young professional, you may not be overly concerned about retirement. But you need to start building toward it eventually. Look for plans that allow you to become vested quickly, so that when you change companies, you'll have a pool of money to reinvest in your future.
- **Education benefits**—Does the company pay for part or all of school and job-related seminar expenses? This can be worth thousands of dollars if you are planning to pursue advanced degrees. It's also an indication of the value the organization places on continued education.
- **Parking**—This may or may not be an issue. But in many metropolitan areas parking can cost hundreds of dollars per year. If so, you need to find out who pays for it.

It's essential to get all offers in writing, especially if you have negotiated any special conditions. For example, suppose your new boss has agreed to give you a special six-month review after you start work. If that guarantee isn't stated in your offer letter, it doesn't mean much. Remember, people sometimes promise more than they can deliver. By getting it in writing you protect yourself.

It can take from two days to six weeks after the interview to receive an offer package. This generally consists of an offer letter stating the position, the salary, a tentative starting date, any special conditions that were agreed to, and a brochure describing standard company benefits. There are usually two originals of the letter. You signify your acceptance by signing one and returning it by a certain date. The other is for your records.

If you are working, never give notice until you receive your new offer in writing. When you're ready to give notice, write a brief letter to your boss. Thank him or her for the opportunities you've been given, and clearly state your last work day. No matter how you feel on the inside, never burn bridges. It's a small world, and you never know when you may need another job or who you will end up working for in the future.

Your letter of resignation might go something like this:

Your home address and phone number
The ABC Company
Attention: James Smith, Supervisor
Gizmo Department
Anytown, USA

Dear Mr. Smith:

I hereby resign from the ABC Company effective July 1, 1995. This is not a decision I have made lightly, but I believe the new position I have accepted is more in line with my qualifications and the direction I wish to take in my career.

I would, however, like to take this opportunity to thank you, management, and my co-workers for a rewarding and satisfying work experience.

I have enjoyed my three years with the gizmo department, and I wish the organization continued success.

Sincerely,

It's important to include your home address to ensure that the human resources department can later send you any tax or termination papers you may need.

After you've signed up, no matter how much homework you've done, you'll still be the new kid on the block. Succeeding in the workplace, like landing a job, is more than a matter of enthusiasm: It involves knowing what people want and honing your skills to provide it.

Chapter 6

SURVIVING AND THRIVING IN THE WORKPLACE

You got a job. That's great, but where in the world are you? Just like people, companies come in all shapes, sizes, and personalities. In addition to identifying and understanding the corporate structure of your company, you need to understand the people who work there. You also need to master corporate policies and politics: Explicit rules are policy, and unwritten rules are politics.

Whether you work with 2 or 200 people, politics are going to be part of the equation. Being politically savvy can help you give companies what they want, and it helps you get what you want in return—without sacrificing your dignity or integrity.

WHAT CORPORATE AMERICA VALUES

Companies are more sensitive than ever to the bottom line. They want employees who can help to improve it in a very short time. It used to be that if you had great credentials, a company might hire you without a specific position in mind—a sort of "stockpiling talent" mentality. The conventional wisdom was that you could ultimately fit in somewhere.

Now organizations are looking for more effectiveness and

efficiency. Top executives in all industries are saying, "We have problems, and we need people who can contribute to the solution." Employees are given less time to come up to speed. Companies want someone who can come in and get going.

This doesn't necessarily mean you need lots of experience, but it does mean you need a "can do" attitude and good work habits. "We value risk-takers," says Antonio Otero, director of manufacturing engineering and quality at General Motors. "We want someone who says, "Yes, I can handle that. Yes, I can do that.'"

Otero adds, "In today's corporate environment, companies are looking for diversity—not the specialists we used to seek. We need people who are more flexible, who are able and willing to try different things. An engineer, for example, who can manage, market, or even handle finances."

Companies also want and value people who:

- share the company's goals and objectives
- project the company's image
- understand its products, goals, markets, and customers
- have flexibility and a range of skills
- are persistent, reliable, thorough, and able to meet deadlines
- demonstrate initiative and a good grasp of what needs to be done without overly close supervision
- can communicate both orally and in writing
- are enthusiastic and have a positive attitude
- are congenial and cooperative
- are team players
- demonstrate a willingness to keep up-to-date in their fields

- care about quality
- leave personal problems at home
- don't act like know-it-alls
- don't watch the clock

GIVE THEM WHAT THEY WANT

Success doesn't just happen, but there is no secret or magic behind it, either. It starts with taking responsibility for yourself. "Given a reasonably level playing field, which most companies in the U.S. are striving to achieve, it is up to the individual to perform as well as he or she can, to persevere, and to gain confidence that in the end, excellent performance will win out," says Dr. Arnold F. Stancell, the first African-American vice president at Mobil Corporation.

But, he notes, "It takes more than just intellectual smarts." He should know. From humble beginnings in Harlem to the boardroom of an international giant, Stancell compiled an impressive list of accomplishments: scientist, businessman, communicator, and teacher. When Stancell won the 1992 Black Engineer of the Year Award, Allen E. Murray, chairman and chief executive office at Mobil, said, "He turned adversity into challenge, and obstacles into opportunities."

Stancell's recipe for success is simple. "Never stop learning," he says. "You have to understand how things work; for example, the culture of the company. Learn how to speak effectively and communicate in all directions—upward, downward, and sideways. Learn when to listen and when to speak. Understand teamwork and learn to be a team player. This may require you to subdue some individualism or to channel it properly. Learn to be a controlled risk-taker. Learn to identify opportunities where you can show that you have the right stuff. These are all things you can do for yourself."

BASIC POLITICS

Nonminorities sometimes believe that minorities don't understand workplace politics or know how to play and win. Prove them wrong. Here's how:

- **Know the company culture.** From dress to decision-making, be aware of your environment and which company customs are acceptable. For example, some companies make decisions by committee. In others, key managers make decisions. Knowing how your organization operates can help you successfully push new ideas or programs.

- **Never make the boss look bad.** This is always a sure way to fall into political disfavor and end up a loser. Do everything you can (within reason) to support your boss and enhance his or her image.

- **Identify the people with power.** Every organization has movers and shakers. Learn who they are and how they operate. If possible, try to develop good relationships with them.

- **Be a straight shooter.** Honor commitments and follow through. This includes being loyal to the company and the people in the company. Deviousness can backfire.

- **Be visible.** If you are always buried in your work area, you won't get the exposure you need. Get involved in activities that make you visible to management. Being seen after normal working hours is also a plus. Staying at work an extra half hour can pay dividends, since managers usually stay late and will notice who is still there.

- **Learn to say yes.** Don't promise impossible results, but be willing to tackle tough assignments. It sends the message that you are a doer.
- **Be responsible.** Don't blame others unless something that went wrong was clearly not your fault.
- **Don't be a complainer.** If something is wrong, try to make it better. Complaining doesn't fix problems; action does.
- **Show humility, but don't be a doormat.** Strike a balance. No one likes a braggart or someone who is too cocky. But being too laid-back also sends the wrong message.
- **Listen more than you speak.** You'll learn more that way, and others will respect you more. And when you do speak, people will take you more seriously.
- **Treat everyone with respect and consideration.** That means not only those in your peer group and people above you in the corporate structure but those below you as well.
- **Give credit where credit is due.** Nothing undermines your political strength faster than taking credit that belongs to someone else. It can cause resentment and disloyalty.
- **Develop an internal network.** You already developed an external network when you were job-hunting. Now you need to build one within your company. Integrating your network is crucial; for more on this subject, see Chapter 8.
- **If you want to promote an idea, involve others.**

Nothing makes people more supportive than being asked to contribute and participate. It also reduces the risk to you.

- **Be indispensable.** Seek key assignments and perform so well that your supervisors can't imagine the organization being successful without you.

- **Offer your help or resources to co-workers before you ask for something in return.** Helping to shoulder burdens with others creates strong bonds.

- **Listen to the grapevine.** Don't, however, repeat irresponsible rumors and gossip. Carefully evaluate what you hear and act accordingly.

- **Don't be afraid to admit you're not perfect.** Saying "I don't know" or "I need help" is not a crime. Neither is making an occasional mistake.

- **Learn to use the system.** Fighting corporate bureaucracy is usually fruitless. Work within the system and try to effect positive change from the inside. You'll accomplish more.

- **Avoid loud confrontations.** Never engage in a shouting match with anyone. And never engage in personal attacks.

- **Handle criticism constructively.** Listen to what is being said. If it doesn't have merit, try to set the record straight. If it does, take action to correct the problem.

- **Learn restraint.** Tolerate the shortcomings and inconsistencies of others. Never overreact, and don't criticize unless you can make it constructive.

Be Careful What You Say

Susan never liked Mary, who supervised another section in the company's finance division. In fact, she thought Mary was an "insufferable, racist idiot." Unfortunately, she made the mistake of telling a friend, who told another co-worker. Susan's opinion of Mary got back to her. Mary eventually arranged to have Susan transferred to her section. As Susan's new supervisor, she put so much pressure on her that she quit after two months. The moral: No matter how large or small the organization, never bad-mouth anyone. You never know who you will end up working for or with.

Network Power

Jesse was the first African American the company hired to work in its strategic planning group. He quickly became respected for his hard work and professionalism. Still, there was an undercurrent of resentment against him among some group members. One day in the company cafeteria, Jesse started talking to an older white man. Over the next several weeks they chatted about everything from the local elections to sports. Jesse learned that his new friend, Randall, was the director of the operations department.

Jesse maintained his lunchtime talks with Randall on a fairly regular basis. Six months later Jesse was under consideration for a promotion. He mentioned it to Randall. It turned out that the boss who would be making the final selection was a friend of Randall's. He offered to put a good word in for Jesse. He pulled his personnel file, liked what he saw, and followed through. Jesse got the promotion.

Discovered

Bob was known as a hard-charging manager who arrived early and worked late. When the company president asked him to head a special task force, he immediately began to staff it with people he respected and trusted.

> **Success doesn't just happen, but there is no secret or magic behind it, either.**

On his way to after-hours meetings with the president, Bob often saw Richard working alone at his desk. Finally he asked another manager, "Who's that guy I always see working late in the finance department?"

"That's Richard. He's been here about six months now. Super worker."

Bob pulled his personnel file and checked Richard's record. Impressed with what he saw, he approached Richard's boss and asked if he could "steal" Richard for several months to work on his task force. Richard took advantage of the opportunity to work on Bob's special project and eventually went to work for the senior manager permanantly.

COMMUNICATION AND IMAGE: PROJECTING THE RIGHT STUFF

Like it or not, your success depends in large part not on performance but image. Many career-management experts say you'll never succeed in corporate America if you don't look the part. As a minority, you have to develop a balance between your heritage and personal style and what companies want and expect from you. If you want to create a favorable, lasting impression, you must maintain a consistently professional image—from the way you carry yourself and dress to your speech, attitude, and demeanor.

The office is not the place to make a style statement. Acceptable dress will obviously vary by geography, industry, and job type. You need to study your surroundings and learn what is appropriate. A good time to do that is during your interview, *before* you start on the job. (What you should wear *at* the interview is discussed in Chapter 5.)

For instance, if you work in a bank in Philadelphia, a suit may be the only thing to wear. If, however, you work at a computer company in California, it may be perfectly acceptable to wear jeans and a sweatshirt. Generally, though, when it comes to appearance, it's best to err on the conservative side. This means not only avoiding innapropriate clothing, but also wild hairstyles or excessive jewelry.

By conforming to company dress codes and standards, you're showing management that you understand what is expected. You're also projecting an impression of compatibility with those expectations. You may love trendy colors and flashy jewelry, but work is not the place to indulge those tastes. Save them for your leisure time.

In an effort to assert their ethnic identity, some minorities reject standard business attire in favor of less traditional alternatives. They may feel flattered by the attention co-workers give them for their independence, but they aren't thrilled when they're passed over for promotions or challenging assignments because they've sent the wrong signals.

"Managers want people who not only are good at what they

do but who also convey the company image," says an African-American executive with a Chicago-based plastics company. He adds, "When I first came to work, I saw skilled people who dressed incorrectly passed over when it came time to send out a representative to make a presentation or to market a client. Although this struck me right away, it wasn't until later, when I was passed over for a promotion, that I began to look at myself. I now understand "corporate uniforms,' and I believe this awareness has been important to my success. Proper dress is part of projecting a winning image." Still, he cautions, "dress is certainly no substitute for competence."

Creating a winning image goes beyond clothes. View it as a complete package, including credibility, authority, self-confidence, and, of course, the way you express yourself.

COMMUNICATION: TALK IS CHEAP

Abraham Lincoln said, "It is better to keep silent and let people think you are a fool than to open your mouth and remove all doubt." That may be true; but unless you are a monk or a hermit, you have to communicate. If it's time to speak up and you don't, your silence will say a lot about you—most of it negative.

Whether you're speaking to one person, a small group, or a conference room full of people, you need to be understood. Almost nothing contributes to creating an image of competence like the ability to communicate well. If you're not an effective speaker, you should take steps to improve your skills. Doing so costs nothing but commitment and desire.

How to Make Them Listen

You can project a better image by working on how you sound and how you deliver words. That doesn't mean you have to take voice lessons or change yourself. It does mean enhancing what you have.

"Have you ever read a children's story out loud?" asks Lucie Eggleston, a prominent consultant who specializes in improving the presentation and writing skills of others. She explains, "If you have, you probably used a lot of vocal variety. If you haven't, try it. Reading a kid's story brings out that capability—we slow down, we speed up, we pause, and we change tone and pitch."

When you perform this experiment, tape it. It will give you instant feedback about how you sound to others. Most of us are a little shocked when we first hear a recording of our own voice. If you don't like what you hear, use a tape recorder and work to develop a better sound.

Always use the three C's when you speak: Present points clearly, crisply, and creatively. And keep in mind these other dos and don'ts for improving speech basics.

- **Don't use slang or raw language.** Almost nothing will destroy your professional image faster than the use of street language in the office. And using crude or vulgar language is even worse. Even if you graduated at the top of your college class, to others you'll sound as if you never went to school.

- **Enunciate clearly.** Take time to pronounce each word carefully if you want people to listen to you and understand what you're saying. If you have an accent that prevents people from clearly understanding you, get out your tape recorder or talk to a friend and work to improve your understandability. That doesn't mean you have to lose either your accent or your second language.

- **Keep it simple.** Don't complicate things. Get to the point and stick to the subject.
- **Say what you mean.** Don't be ambiguous; be straightforward. Use clear language, not jargon.
- **Be diplomatic.** Speak your mind with tact. If you're upset or angry, don't speak until you feel in control of your emotions.
- **Build a vocabulary and use it.** Give up five minutes of TV viewing a day and use the time to browse through the dictionary. Learn one new word a day.
- **Maintain eye contact with the person or audience you are talking to.**
- **Gesture effectively.** Contrary to what you may have heard, powerful individuals usually keep their hands still when they speak. When they do gesture, it is meaningful and deliberate. Study effective speakers and their gestures.
- **Set yourself apart from the crowd with more than words.** For example, if during a conference your colleagues ask questions from their auditorium seats, stand up when you ask yours. Also, avoid interrupting others.

Overcoming the Shakes

You may handle yourself just fine one-on-one or in small, informal meetings. But if you are like most people, you may experience very real jitters when it comes to addressing large groups. That's normal. In a survey included in *The Book of*

Lists, fear of public speaking outranked the fear of death by a two-to-one margin. But you don't have to be scared speechless. There are effective ways to overcome it.

One of the most effective ways is to join a speakers' club such as Toastmasters International. (Refer to the appendix for information on finding your local chapter.) Such groups offer a learn-by-doing environment that allows you to develop skills in a friendly atmosphere. Members progress though a series of speaking assignments, after which fellow members evaluate them and offer concrete recommendations for improvement.

Improved public-speaking skills can result in higher salaries and professional advancement. They undoubtedly lead to increased self-confidence and poise. And joining a speakers' club is an excellent way to network.

Secrets of Successful Speakers

Have you ever heard someone give an outstanding presentation? If you have, you'll recognize these elements:

- **Involvement** with and from the audience
- **Creativity** in approach and use of media
- **Flow** from start to finish; smooth structure and organization
- **Flexibility** of style and content to adapt to different groups
- **Polish** in voice, gestures, and demeanor

No matter how well-spoken you are, verbal skills are only half of what you need to stand apart as an effective communicator in the business world. You must also be able to express yourself on paper.

GO WRITE AHEAD

Contrary to popular belief, writing well doesn't come naturally, even to "born writers." As with any other endeavor, practice makes perfect.

How you write is often as important as what you write. If your writing skills are lacking when you start a new job, you may have to rely on a co-worker to review your writing before it goes out or gets routed through the boss's office. But for the long term, you need to take a company-sponsored writing workshop or attend an evening session at the local college.

Most young professionals put off taking steps to improve their writing skills. It's no fun sitting in night school after a hard day at the office. But it's just like achieving financial success: You can't expect dividends unless you invest. In this case you're investing your time and energy in a skill that will pay off in future success.

Managers hate to see unclear, poorly written reports and memos. It's a waste of time to plow through several pages just to glean one or two ideas that could have been stated in one or two paragraphs. Don't be among those who stall their careers by failing to develop good writing skills. Learn the secrets of successful business writers. This starts with developing a consistent approach and good habits.

- **Make a list** of your ideas. Don't try to write complete sentences. Just get it all out by jotting down key words and phrases.
- **Review and arrange.** After you have poured your ideas out on paper, go back and arrange them in logical order. If you've written a lot and you aren't using a personal com-

puter to move text around, you might take scissors and cut up your list and tape it together in the right order.

- **Expand on your ideas** and write the document. Flesh out ideas and turn words into sentences. Try to do this in a single sitting if possible, so you don't lose your train of thought. Don't forget who your audience is. Use the active rather than the passive voice. Write "Remove the disk before turning off the computer," not "The disk should be removed before the computer is turned off." Don't worry too much about grammar or misspelled words at this stage. And don't be creative when it comes to format. If the company has an established structure for memos, for example, follow it.

"Managers want people who not only are good at what they do but who also convey the company image."

- **Edit.** A sentence (like most people's checkbook balance) seldom comes out right the first time, or even the second or third time. Rewrite and edit, then edit some more. Be sure your thoughts flow logically. Remove every excess word you can find. Check punctuation. After you have "polished up" your document, review it one more time.

THE LIKABILITY FACTOR

If you ask a manager or executive, "Did you ever hire or promote someone you didn't like?" the answer will most likely be no. Senior officials admit they often choose one candidate over another for something they call the "likability factor." Actually, it makes sense. Your boss is apt to spend almost as much time with you as with his or her family. Therefore, compatibility is crucial.

Of course, likability is subjective. But there are some basics:

- **Smile.** It's the easiest and most important way to project likability. And it makes you and everyone around you feel good.
- **Project a positive, self-confident attitude.** But don't come across as self-centered or superior.
- **Be friendly.** If you're shy by nature, work to overcome it. That means taking even casual opportunities to engage others in conversation. Always seek common ground— whether it's a work project or the fate of the local sports team—as a means to establish communication. Take an interest in what other people care about.
- **Don't forget to laugh.** Nothing keeps things in perspective like seeing the humor in situations. That doesn't mean you have to be the office clown, but it does mean not being overly serious.
- **Respect others.** They'll reciprocate. Remember, it's the little things that count. For example, when visitors come into your office, greet them on your feet.

Positive Motivation

Criticism often comes too easily. You know from your own

experience that a word of praise does a lot more to motivate you. We all like to hear a kind word or a compliment.

Pass it on. Be on the lookout for opportunities to make positive or encouraging remarks about others' work. Use their names when giving praise. Say nice things about people behind their backs, too. Hearing positive comments through a third party always feels great.

The saying "you get what you give" still holds true. If you want others to appreciate your efforts, you need to appreciate theirs. This will go a long way toward creating a positive image. One note of caution, though: Avoid complimenting others on non-work-related issues, such as appearance or dress—especially members of the opposite sex. It could be misinterpreted.

TALES FROM THE EXECUTIVE SUITE

We all tend to see ourselves in the best possible light. But we need to consider how others see us. Heed warning signs that you're not projecting the right image.

Dressed to Kill

"Elena was the best loan officer in the office," says Dave, the manager of a Seattle mortgage company. "When I promoted her to head the department, I was sure she would do a great job. She did. Unfortunately, there was another problem.

"After the promotion she stopped wearing business attire and started coming to the office in what I can only describe as party dresses. She looked great for a wedding or a cocktail party but not appropriate for the office."

Dave asked a more senior female employee to talk to her about toning down her outfits. But Elena remained convinced that she should dress up in keeping with her new position, and she didn't heed the advice. Soon after, Dave was transferred to another office. Immediately, the new manager wanted to know the story on Elena. "Why in the world is that woman managing that department?" he asked. "It's obvious she doesn't understand her job."

Before the situation could be resolved, the office was merged with another, and Elena was demoted to assistant manager in the new operation. She quit. Later she said, "I was really young and naive. I didn't understand what was expected, but I do now." Elena went on to become the manager of the loan department for a bank.

Scared Speechless

Everything was going Ron's way. Throughout college he had spent summers and semester breaks working for the federal government in a work-study program. One of his champions was Marsha, a member of the senior executive service. So, not surprisingly, after Ron earned his degree, he was hired into civil service as an economist.

Under Marsha's guidance he progressed more quickly than his peer group. After three years Marsha felt Ron was ready to assume significant responsibilities. When the agency was asked to study a proposed European-American trade agreement and prepare a report to Congress, Marsha put Ron in charge of the effort.

During one of the first major meetings, Ron rose to give a presentation. What happened next humiliated Ron and embarrassed his sponsor. Ron had prepared his material carefully, but he had never addressed a large group before. When he looked out at the audience, he drew a blank and panicked. Finally, he started speaking in a halting voice. His anxiety grew and he began to stutter and mumble. Somehow he got through the experience, but he was shaken.

He sat down with Marsha and expressed his frustration. They both agreed that Ron would still run the effort. But they also agreed that someone else would handle all subsequent briefings until Ron was ready. It took over four months of work with a local speakers' club, but Ron was finally able to stand with confidence before groups and deliver the goods.

Polishing your skills to meet and exceed corporate expectations is an ongoing process. It takes time and effort, but the career payoffs can be enormous.

Chapter 7

AVOIDING MINORITY TRAPS AND STEREOTYPES

As a minority, you will have to contend with more than the usual assortment of job challenges. Sooner or later, you'll meet face-to-face with an added burden: negative stereotyping.

It's hard to gauge how widespread unfavorable stereotypes about minorities are, but we've all heard them. Lazy. Unmotivated. Untrustworthy. Less intelligent. You know they're nonsense, but how can you dispel them?

Misconceptions about minorities often stem from fear or lack of exposure; the increasing presence of minorities in the workplace should eventually work to diminish them. In the meantime, the best way to deal with bias is to perform at a level that's beyond reproach. Unfair as it is, you may be held to a higher standard than your co-workers. Show that you know what it takes: teamwork, dedication, growth, a keen grasp of office politics, intellectual curiosity, and the ability to develop innovative solutions to complex problems. In a word, professionalism.

"Early on in my career, I became a student for what would be a lifetime study of successful professionals and how they handle projects and people," says a senior manager with a large pharmaceutical company. The 58-year-old African American says, "Based on what I have seen, I have developed a philosophy that has served me well. Sure, there have been times in my career when I've been the object of discrimination, but by not dwelling on the imperfections of others or of the marketplace and by following basics, I have achieved the level of success I sought."

He adds, "As minorities we must control our actions and be responsible for them. The world is not always fair. That's a given. But we can't sit around wringing our hands and worrying about it. I'm often treated with skepticism or dismissed by the young minorities I reach out to help because they think my approach is too simplistic or naive. It's not. It works. I'm proof of that."

> **The best way to deal with bias is to perform at a level that's beyond reproach.**

His philosophy? "There is no real secret to effectively applying your skills. Always do a good job; everything else will usually tend to fall into place. Learn as much as you can about the job. Admit when you are wrong. Correct the situation and go on. Anything else is counterproductive. There are going to be managers and co-workers who won't take you seriously. But through striving to meet high performance standards, you can instill in them the realization that they can trust you and that you can do the job."

DIVERSITY AND CONFORMITY

What corporate America wants to know is that you share its

values of hard work and quality, even if you don't share the same culture. Accommodating cultural diversity requires a certain amount of compromise on both sides, but that doesn't mean you have to sell out. What it does mean is not dragging every aspect of your culture into the office.

Too many minorities associate a measure of conformity with restriction of freedom and self-expression, perhaps even a loss of culture and traditions. That's not so. Workplace culture needs to be standardized because it is based on cooperation. "Your job and career are only part of your lifestyle," says an African-American executive with the nation's largest department-store chain. "There are a total of 168 hours in a week. If you spend 40 hours on the job, that leaves a lot of personal time to express and celebrate your heritage. Competing in corporate America doesn't have to mean compromising ethnic pride and dignity. It does, however, mean fitting within the broad framework of acceptable behavior and image when you are working as part of a team."

When you use the system, you are not selling out. Rather, you are buying into corporate America by adopting certain standards. By not remaining on the fringe, you will be in a better position to use your ethnic identity to influence the system and effect positive change for yourself and others who follow.

> **"Don't contribute to the building of invisible barriers, which exist at too many companies."**

"Don't contribute to the building of invisible barriers,

which exist at too many companies," says Jerry Pitts, director of equal employment opportunity and affirmative action programs at the Martin Marietta Astronautics Group.

> **Judge all discrimination on the basis of its seriousness and its effect on you.**

You tend to attract people who are similar to you. If you don't want to spend time with racists, don't be one. Along the way, don't use the fact that companies now embrace cultural diversity as an excuse to be outrageous. That can be the kiss of death. You will always be perceived as less threatening if you are a team player.

Arnold Stancell of Mobil Corporation advises young professionals, "Address fears head on and neutralize them. Don't be your own worst enemy. There are enough traps out there without adding to them."

AVOIDING CORPORATE TRAPS

With a little planning and effort, most minority snares can be avoided or even turned into assets. Here are some of the common traps:

Tokenism

Tokenism tends to emphasize differences instead of embracing them. It is often a way for organizations to acknowledge and then forget discrimination. Examples of tokenism include hiring or promoting a minority to satisfy pressure from the government or company executives, or using a minority employee as an example of what the organization considers appropriate behavior.

As a token, you may be rewarded with a prestigious title and good pay. Nevertheless, tokenism can end up working to your disadvantage, isolating you on the job not only from other minorities but from the rest of the organization.

Consider Tony's experience. When his company instituted a program aimed at giving minorities preference for certain management training positions, the Japanese American was among the first to express an interest. After his promotion, though, co-workers' resentment made it almost impossible for Tony to succeed. They felt he only made it because he was a minority, although Tony was on a fast track anyway and would probably have achieved this level on his own.

Although co-workers' protests that you benefited from tokenism can jeopardize your position, you can survive and win. First, always do a conscientious job. Never give anyone a chance to force you out for poor performance. Take on as much responsibility as you can. This will tend to legitimize your position. And don't think of yourself as a token, but rather as a trailblazer.

After you have consolidated your position, act. Keep building and strengthening your internal company network. Start trying to bring other minorities into the organization. Don't play overly aggressive or in-your-face politics, but be a firm advocate for change. Find openings or define new roles that you can help fill with minorities. It may not happen overnight, but odds are you won't be a token for long.

The Ethnic Club

Ethnic professional societies or associations can be valuable resources for networking and news about industry trends and training opportunities. And ethnic groups or clubs within companies can provide solid support and information. Most national or regional professional groups are recognized for what they are: groups of people who share a common profession, working together to promote their interests. But beware of associations that are not legitimate social or professional groups. Clubs that promote radical ideas have the potential to alienate a lot of people.

Think about the extreme for a moment. How would you feel about a group called the U.S. White Society of whatever? Your first reaction might very well be negative. Now put yourself in a nonminority's shoes. It's not difficult to understand how clubs based exclusively on race or culture can polarize people and hurt your professional growth.

The Clan

Minorities in organizations tend to stick together both on the job and in social settings. That's normal, but excessive clannishness sets you apart from the rest of your co-workers. You won't be seen as a team player, and you'll miss out on many opportunities to develop important professional and personal relationships.

If you set yourself apart from the rest of the company, you'll never change anything. "We are losing the full use and contribution of some fine minds in technology and leadership positions simply because they don't really join the organization," says Arnold Stancell. "They think it's just talk, or politics, or "kissing up.' That's just not true. It's leadership and all part of growing and becoming more valuable to the organization."

He cautions, "Just as minorities don't want to be the target of prejudice, nonminorities don't want to be the target of negative feelings. You can't be biased the other way." He says, "Have an open mind and be interested in others. Quite frankly, some people are inhibited around those of a different race. Perhaps they are afraid of being rejected."

His advice? "Get rid of all that baggage and look for the best in people. There is always common ground. Reach out, find it, and build on it."

Limited Networking

Another major pitfall is distinct from but related to clannishness. It's not racial bias per se, but rather network bias. "The reality of life in America is that if you are white, most of the people you know are white," says an African-American executive officer with one of the country's largest food-processing companies. "If someone says to you, "Do you know anyone for the job?' the people you recommend will probably be white."

Keeping an integrated network is as important now as it was when you were job hunting. "To be successful, minorities must tap into nonminority networks," according to Stancell. "Don't wait for others. Take the initiative to reach out first. If you do, eventually people will begin to think, "That person is certainly nice to be around.' That's the foundation of network building. Once you start to build those types of relationships, take time to enhance them—call for lunch, show an interest."

Language

Knowing a second language can be an asset at some companies. If you use it to shut others out or tell secrets, it can cause problems. You may be perceived as an outsider, and those who can't understand what you're saying will probably resent you.

"Use your second-language skills as an asset, not as a way to alienate others," says GM's Antonio Otero. "Everything has its place, and that includes when and how you use a foreign language."

Hypersensitivity

Co-workers who are polite or nice to you don't necessarily like you or look out for your best interests when you are out of sight. On the other hand, don't be too sensitive to those who aren't especially nice. Don't assume that racism is behind every negative comment from a nonminority. If you overreact, your anger will keep you on the defensive and unable to learn from what may be constructive criticism.

Success requires learning to keep your emotions balanced. Consider each interaction on a case-by-case basis. This may mean ignoring racial slights and innuendo when they have no bearing on attaining your goals.

STEREOTYPE AND MYTH BUSTERS

Strong networks and support groups can help, but in the end the burden is on you to dispel others' misconceptions and make them see your worth. Work hard at creating the right chemistry in the workplace. Here are some ways to make it happen:

- **Don't allow yourself to become mired at the bottom of the organization.** Actively seek new opportunities and challenges.
- **Monitor your environment.** Develop an awareness of what is going on around you. For instance, a co-worker who is cool toward you may be harboring overt or subconscious biases. Try to uncover these fears or prejudices and act to change them.
- **Give them more than they ask for.** Exceed the minimum standards of your job.
- **Pay your dues.** Many nonminorities are resentful and believe that minorities receive special treatment. Pay your dues and then what can they say?
- **Show enthusiasm.** Bringing energy to your work will help overcome others' indifference or hostility.
- **Don't let your emotions cloud your vision.** Understand your reaction to conflict and, if possible, channel your anger and frustration into positive action.
- **Allay their fears by valuing corporate goals.** Let co-workers see your commitment to getting the job done right and on time, providing quality goods and services, and ensuring the success of the organization.
- **Reach out and become involved with nonminorities.** Get involved in company social and volunteer activities. Don't be an isolationist.
- **Participate in cultural diversity workshops and training.** Through communication you can change peoples' perceptions.

There will always be a few hard-core racists with closed minds. These people will never change. But if you have a positive influence on the majority of nonminorities, you will overcome bias and negative stereotyping. Your objective is not to turn someone who's against you (or who believes in negative stereotypes) into an avid supporter. Rather, in most cases all you need to do is reduce that person's negativity enough so that it doesn't hinder your career.

Don't assume that all minorities will like and help you. They won't. That's why it's important to take responsibility for yourself. By doing so, you will have an impact on other minorities; your success will change things for those who follow.

HANDLING BIAS

You really need to know yourself and your goals to deal with bias effectively. When faced with it, you must ask yourself:

- Is it worth paying attention to? (For example, it might be something petty, like a co-worker's bad attitude. Or it might be more serious, such as discrimination by your boss.)
- Can I do anything to change it?
- Does it bother me so much that it's affecting my performance or standing in the organization?
- Am I using it as an excuse not to achieve my goals?
- Do the benefits of fighting back outweigh the political costs?

Consider how Edward handled Paula, a co-worker who constantly made slurs against Latinos. Edward ignored the comments and continued to build a solid work record. Eventually he was promoted and became Paula's boss. He then took steps to correct the situation.

Anita, on the other hand, took every slur personally and

responded by getting into shouting matches with a co-worker who made his feelings toward Hispanics known. On more than one occasion, she complained to company management. She never did this formally, though. Gradually she developed the reputation for being too sensitive and was passed over for a significant promotion.

Who's right? Who's wrong? That depends on the situation and on you. Judge all discrimination on the basis of its seriousness and its effect on you. If there's a strong pattern of bias, fighting may be advisable. If, however, discrimination or ethnic slurs occur infrequently, you should ask yourself if taking action will prevent you from reaching your career goals. In other words, know the consequences before you take action. (Chapter 9 discusses how to take formal action if you feel discrimination warrants it.)

TALES FROM THE FRONT LINES

Seeds of Change

Sam had worked at the North Carolina plant for over 15 years. When he started out, there was very little automation, but in the past two years the company had merged three separate operations into an automated manufacturing facility. Instead of just line workers, he now supervised spare parts, an administrative group, and all the engineers and computer scientists and programmers who made it function.

Philip, a gifted computer scientist, was part of the group Sam inherited from another facility. Sam didn't like the African American from the first time he met him. He felt threatened by Philip and believed he was all image and no substance. As Sam was fond of reminding his friends, "These kinds of guys just don't measure up." Yet Sam knew that management thought Philip was a rising star and that he was stuck with him. Besides, Sam figured, it was a large plant, and he would just limit the contact he had with Philip.

Philip, sensing this dislike, studied his new boss carefully. He knew his own performance was exceptional, and he couldn't understand why Sam was obviously uncomfortable around him.

After a new batch of control software was installed without proper testing, the whole line went down on a Monday night. When Sam was called back to the plant, he was surprised to find Philip already trying to solve the problem. Aside from the operations side, Sam knew nothing about computers. He felt frustrated as he watched Philip tap on the computer keyboard and fill the screen with data.

Then a good thing happened. Sam started asking questions. Philip went out of his way to explain what he was doing in layman's terms. Sam's knowledge of the overall operation prompted him to start asking "what if?" questions. Before long, they were working as a team. Philip could sense that Sam had begun to see him in a new light.

At 1:30 a.m., after the problem was solved and things were restored to normal, Philip offered to buy Sam breakfast at an all-night coffee shop, and the two men talked. Sam asked Philip how he knew so much about computers, and even hinted that he may have misjudged Philip. He also thanked Philip for taking the time to help solve the problem.

It was the first step to a new relationship, though the change didn't happen overnight. First came mutual respect; eventually, they became friends both on and off the job.

Stuck with Each Other

Rosaline had fought the reorganization, but it happened anyway. She was determined to make the best of it, even though her billing department had been aligned under the corporate VP in charge of finance, Ben, who was rumored to dislike Hispanics and women professionals in general, dismissing them as an inconvenience in a man's world.

At first he tried to micromanage her operation. He seemed to take delight in undermining her authority and dismissing her management initiatives as trivial. Rosaline grew increasingly frustrated but didn't lose her head. She kept trying.

When company profits started to dip, management began to look at areas of the company that could use improvement. One area was cash flow. As the overall boss for finances, Ben was the focus of criticism from the senior brass for failing to institute more innovative billing procedures. At one critical meeting, attended by both Ben and Rosaline, Ben was grilled about why personal computers weren't being used to expedite invoices.

Rosaline had been pushing this idea, but Ben had rejected it. Instead of making him look bad in the meeting, however, she said, "Ben and I have been discussing this, and we have a plan to implement a new system. Up to this point, he hasn't felt that the timing was right, but I'm sure he now agrees we should move in that direction."

Surprised that Rosaline hadn't burned him in front of senior management and flustered at being championed by a woman, Ben said, "Yes, that's correct. I'll let Rosaline give you the details." She did, and she and Ben promised to have a full report to the front office by the end of the week. After the meeting Ben went to Rosaline's office and thanked her for her support. Then he asked her flat out why she had reacted so positively. Rosaline told him she wanted to work with him, not against him.

Ben would later tell his boss what a true professional Rosaline was. Respect had been established, and, although they never became personal friends, they worked well together, and Rosaline was able to successfully push other innovative ideas with his support.

Rosaline did something politically astute: She protected the boss. In the process she made herself look good and made Bill see her not just as a minority woman but a talented professional.

In the overwhelming majority of organizations, you can grow professionally and prosper. (Chapter 9 discusses what to do if you aren't allowed to grow because of discrimination.) For minorities and nonminorities alike, however, establishing a solid record of success takes time, commitment, and know-how.

Chapter 8

BUILDING A TRACK
RECORD

The 1990s promise to be a decade marked by a stormy corporate climate. Building a solid record of success and recession-proofing your career will take persistence and dedication to personal excellence. Regardless of your field, moving ahead is more a matter of good judgment than of raw intelligence.

When senior managers at Xerox were asked what advice they would give people who wanted to advance, the top seven responses were:

- show results
- be political; be visible
- take charge of your career
- work hard
- develop a broad range of experiences
- develop strong technical skills
- develop strong interpersonal skills

Unless you own the company, the value of your efforts will be determined by others. That's why you need to make sure that you position yourself smartly to ensure that you are seen as an asset to the organization, not a liability.

Corporations with a history of prospering—even during uncertain times—usually have a no-nonsense approach to business. Young professionals should adopt the same strategy. Even in the best of times, you should take steps to ensure that you are not expendable. By adapting a savvy approach, you can reach your goals during the good times and survive when tough times hit. Here are the key issues you should never overlook as you build and maintain a strong record:

Continually strive to develop unequaled and transferable skills. You have to think in terms of the two extremes: unique and universal. Few things ensure a successful track record like developing uncommon skills or skills that have broad applications. You can do this by tackling unusual tasks or getting specialized training.

> You need a range of skills that will give you the mobility to change companies and even industries.

Stretch yourself and get out of your niche. Become more versatile and able to move with the times. You need skills that will transcend your department, your division, your company, and even your industry. For instance, computer, finance, or marketing skills can often be applied to a wide variety of organizations.

Unfortunately, people tend to let their past predict their future. If you're an accountant, say, you'll probably find your job prospects limited to the accounting industry—unless you obtain broader skills. For example, you might take a course that will help you apply your basic accounting skills to corporate financial operations. Professionals are frequently caught unprepared when there is a recession, a corporate merger, or an industry downturn. Don't paint yourself into a corner.

In today's environment, whether you are just starting out or have gained some hard-earned experience, you would be wise to think both short- and long-term. For the long term, you may want to take steps to improve your credentials and abilities, including not only specialties but essential skills as well. Personnel managers overwhelmingly say that three leading "must haves" for workers of this decade and beyond are computer skills, oral communications, and flexibility.

Top executives, recruiters, and career counselors indicate that the typical career path of the 90s will begin with a couple of years at a corporation where you hone basic skills and start to build a solid network. After that you might move on and start to build a portfolio of skills outside of your core expertise. This could lead to management or a career outside your primary industry. Where you are in the career cycle will determine how you set goals and shape plans.

The key is to maintain mobility and professional flexibility as you develop skills that transcend a particular industry. Forget about titles. You need a range of skills that will give you the mobility to change companies and even industries.

Stay industry-smart. Far too many minorities ignore industry trends, preferring instead to keep a low profile. But when you ignore new developments, you fail to adapt your skills to new needs and risk becoming expendable when the economy sours. Listen to what people are saying and read industry literature, including newsletters and trade journals.

Position yourself properly. Being in the right place at the right time to take advantage of new opportunities is not always easy, but it's within your control. Stay current on emerging profit and power centers and technologies in your company. Be prepared to capitalize on them.

Stay flexible and, again, try to build a portfolio of diverse skills. If you can help the organization in more than one area, you are more likely to be viewed as an asset.

Intracompany moves are often influenced by politics. This means knowing the right managers and what they need, and tailoring your qualifications to fit those needs. It also means staying out of bad spots. Suppose, for example, you are working in gizmo production. You know that sales have been slumping and the company is thinking about cutting back that division. Try to position yourself so that you can move to a healthy division.

> **Never present a problem to the boss without suggesting a constructive solution.**

Never price yourself out of a job or out of the market. When your salary needs or demands exceed the going rate for your job, you're in trouble. Many laid-off professionals have found this out the hard way. You can become overpriced simply by being a steady employee and getting a few annual salary increases. That doesn't mean you should turn down a raise. It does, however, mean you should keep your skills and value at least on a par with your earnings. As your pay increases, so should your skill level and responsibilities. That's another incentive to keep climbing the corporate ladder.

Always strive to improve the company's bottom line. No matter what your job—paper pushing or hardware production—you produce a product. Not understanding your product can quickly get you in trouble. You also need to know the relationship between your efforts and company profits. Too often people say they can't readily put a dollar value on their contributions. For example, you may work in a shipping department, an area that has an indirect influence on the bottom line. Yet it's an essential function. Look for ways to save the company money. Most company managers operate on the philosophy that "if you watch the pennies, the dollars will take care of themselves."

Solicit and give feedback. This starts with building a strong relationship with your boss and understanding his or her goals and problems. Build this relationship on mutual objectives. Solicit feedback on how you can improve your performance and contribute more to the company. Don't wait until you have your six-month or annual performance review to do this; do it on an ongoing basis.

Also, remember that feedback is a two-way street. Identify problems that affect your organization and try to come up with ways to solve them. Most professionals say you should never present a problem to the boss without being able to suggest a constructive solution. Seek feedback from co-workers, especially senior professionals. They may be able to point out aspects of your performance that could use improvement.

Start (and maintain) a career log that lists your activities and accomplishments. This can be an extremely useful tool when you go in for your formal performance review. Your log should also include what you'd like to accomplish. Use it as a reminder to yourself and a basis for goal-setting with your boss during performance reviews.

When you do sit down with the boss to discuss your performance, make sure he or she is aware of all of your achievements. If you are required to sign an evaluation, do so, but with a short note describing any inaccuracies. Generally, if you have been exchanging feedback with your supervisor over the course of the evaluation period, there won't be any surprises. (Chapter 9 discusses how good records can help if you face job discrimination.)

Keep both internal and external networks on-line. It's worth mentioning again because networking is so vital to career success and advancement. Many professionals fail to keep networking when their careers are prospering and they don't feel their job security is threatened. But you should make the effort to stay in touch with contacts outside the organization and continue strengthening relationships with those inside the company.

Don't just concentrate on your peer group. Aim higher as well. Remember, the top power structure in most companies still consists of white males, so work on strengthening your nonminority network. Often those contacts can help you get a promotion or make your career prosper. Plan to meet one new person a month by participating in workshops, seminars, and volunteer activities.

Adopt a mentor. A knowledgeable senior mentor can give you valuable advice and guidance, help you extend your network upward in the organization, and help you develop effective political skills. One word of caution, though: Never tie yourself so tightly to a mentor that your star rises or falls on his or her fate. Identifying too strongly with one person or one crowd can shut you out of other groups and opportunities. Complement the value of mentors by seeking other successful role models.

Take risks. After you get to know your organization, you should be able to see where the action is. Sometimes opportunity will strike quickly; be prepared to say yes and step in. Volunteer and make a point of expressing interest in high-visibility assignments. If you aren't senior enough to manage such a job, get close to someone who can, so that when he or she takes on a big project, you are in a position to be part of the team and share the credit.

But don't be suicidal. There's a difference between a challenging assignment and an impossible one. For example, be wary of tasks that other talented professionals have tried and failed to accomplish. If such tasks then come to you (or you volunteer for them), make certain you know how to succeed. Always be sure you are given the time, power, and resources required to do the job. If not, don't even try it.

Taking on too much can be a trap. Rhonda found this out the hard way. A technical writer for a northern California electronics firm, Rhonda was on a fast track. When the schedule for developing and writing operating and maintenance manuals for a major government contract fell behind schedule, she stepped forward and told her boss she could fix the problem.

She wasn't that familiar with the specific program, but she felt confident because she had worked to develop technical documentation for what she thought were similar systems. Based on the number of pages and the time remaining, she said she could accomplish the task with a five-person team of writers. Rhonda was given the green light and plunged ahead.

Then she discovered problems. The system was much more complicated than she had expected, and the job had been underbid. After she was already committed, she realized that if she were to bring the problems to management's attention, she would look bad. After all, she had volunteered. She decided she had no choice and made a herculean effort to meet the deadlines. She failed. The company was financially penalized by the government because it hadn't delivered according to the terms of the contract.

Rhonda believed her boss, who had originally bid the job— and grossly underestimated it—had set her up as the fall guy. No matter. Her boss survived, and Rhonda's star was tarnished. Rhonda failed because she made herself responsible without first arming herself with the facts. To start with, she should have gotten a clearer picture of the job by talking to the task manager who initially failed to complete it.

Avoid the Peter Principle. In 1969 Laurence J. Peter published his now-famous Peter Principle: "In a hierarchy, individuals tend to rise to their levels of incompetence." Avoiding this dilemma requires planning and patience. You have to build a real record of success one step at a time.

A top Los Angeles recruiter observes, "There seems to be an absolute compulsion that one must have success now, instead of establishing a sound record. A solid grounding in a range of related skills is paramount. It's relatively easy to cook up a "paper tiger' resume and start chasing a heftier paycheck."

Think of your career as a structure. Tall buildings need strong foundations. The L.A. recruiter adds, "Too often minorities who are educated, bright, and articulate think that they need no additional skills to end up in the executive suite. They're wrong. Then, when it doesn't happen, they cry "foul' or discrimination."

In other words, basic technical competence is a necessary but insufficient condition for advancement. You need to concentrate on building a credible, well-rounded professional foundation, then seek opportunities to acquire leadership skills. For example, direct a fund-raising drive for a charity, or volunteer to head up a company task force. Such activities will help you develop and polish your people skills.

Before taking a promotion, know the job description and what's expected. That includes what's written and what's not. Make a list of your skills and qualifications and see if you can do the job. That doesn't mean it can't be a stretch; there are few perfect matches when it comes to moving up to a higher level in the organization. And you will probably be expected to do some growing into the job. But you should possess the basic skills.

Think of your career as a structure. Tall buildings need strong foundations.

Remember, the higher you go, the more people skills and political savvy you need. And you develop those skills not by earning a bachelor's or master's degree but through on-the-job experience.

Think of your job in terms of satisfaction as well as salary. Pay doesn't really matter much if you hate what you're doing. And if you have gotten yourself in over your head and are not performing well, you will be miserable.

Always wear your parachute. You should always be prepared to answer the question "What would I do if I lost my job today?" That's why you need to continually update your resume, stay abreast of industry trends, and keep your networks on-line.

Always listen for opportunities, even if you are not contemplating a move. Always read employment ads so you are aware of what's available. In other words, no matter how much you like your job or how secure you feel, always be prepared to move with minimal warning. (Chapter 10 explores the dynamics of making both forced and planned changes.)

Avoid controversy. Always display the highest integrity and ethics. Don't try to take shortcuts to the top. If your values clash with the company's, be true to yourself and try to make some changes for the better. That starts with sweating even the small stuff. For example, would you give an official from the city government an expensive gift in order to land a contract? Or is it ethical to use your cousin's company as a vendor?

Think in terms of how your actions could be viewed. Be conservative about where you draw the line. If in doubt, don't do it. And if co-workers are involved in something iffy, do everything in your power to keep from being part of it.

Gary didn't and it almost ruined his career. As the project manager on a contract for the federal government, he was responsible for approving time sheets for labor hours billed to the government. This entailed making sure the right charge numbers were used. When a fellow manager came to him and asked if Gary could cover one of his workers under a charge number until some contract issues were straightened out, Gary said yes. "I knew it was wrong, but I figured it was innocent because the hours would be paid back within a month," he says.

Before the records were adjusted, though, Gary got caught in a routine time-sheet audit. He wasn't prosecuted, but he lost his job, even though he swears the practice of temporarily covering other managers was standard company policy, and even though it was clear that he couldn't have benefited financially from the deal. Gary ended up working as an assistant manager in a retail store for less money. The moral: No matter how innocent something seems, think before you act.

Use the system to your benefit. Watch out for the pitfalls of tokenism (see Chapter 7), but take advantage of other programs aimed at helping minorities, such as educational and other benefits for minorities. Such programs improve your skills without making others feel that you are receiving special treatment or an extra boost up the corporate ladder.

When climbing upward, remember that the higher you go, the less "up" there is. You're not going to be the only one in the world who is able, motivated, and skillful. The closer to the top you are, the more you and your competition will be of about equal competence.

Despite all your planning and efforts, however, things may not always work out because you can't control how people treat you. In such cases you must decide whether it's better to avoid confrontation or face injustices head-on. These are tough personal and professional choices, and you should know the potential benefits and dangers before acting.

Chapter 9

MAKING WAVES: FIGHTING AND SURVIVING DISCRIMINATION

There are no lifetime job guarantees for anyone—not you, me, or the guy down the street. Corporations periodically change directions and priorities. Some changes are due to technological advances; in other cases companies are sold, merged with other organizations, downsized, or relocated. Along the way, people lose jobs and miss out on promotions.

Companies don't owe a living to any employee unless that employee can contribute to production, sales, and customer satisfaction. From the janitor to the top manager, that's true no matter how hard you work or how loyal you are. If you are not perceived as contributing to the corporate bottom line, you are expendable.

That's the reality of the marketplace. Unfortunately, there's another reality: All too frequently minorities lose jobs or lose out on promotions because of discrimination.

Losing your job or being passed over for a promotion can seriously damage both your feelings and your pocketbook. If it happens often enough, it can ruin your career. Even worse, it can drain you of your initiative and make you feel that no matter how hard you work, you are destined to fail or to be stalled at a certain level.

GET THE FACTS

If you are terminated or miss out on a promotion, the first thing to do is stay calm (or as calm as possible). Don't overreact and exhibit behavior that may come back to haunt you. No matter how much it hurts, maintain your dignity and professionalism.

Next, become a detective. It's essential that you find out why it happened. If you were fired, did a whole section or organization disappear? Did your immediate supervisor get laid off too? Does the reduction in force appear to be the result of poor business conditions, slumping company sales, or the loss of a contract? Was the company bought by another organization? Did it merge with a competitor?

Find the answers immediately. Talk to your boss and co-workers. Be honest and direct. Ask why and try to get specifics. If you were fired because of normal changes in business and the marketplace, you should pick up the pieces and get on with finding another job. (See Chapter 10.)

If, however, you were the only one to get fired, company management has an obligation to provide you with an official reason. Ask for it. The main thing to consider is whether employees in your job category who are less senior or less competent than you were retained. If so, you may have been the victim of discrimination—or at the very least poor management.

If you were passed over for a promotion, you also need to find out why. Were you qualified in terms of education, technical expertise, and communication and leadership skills? Were you passed over before? Did someone more qualified or senior get the job?

If you weren't fully qualified, or if a more qualified candidate got the job, you need to make sure you acquire the training and skills to be selected for future promotions. If you were qualified in all respects, however, discrimination may have played a role.

Tough Questions

The most difficult part of evaluating the facts is self-examination. Remember, losing your job or missing out on a promotion doesn't necessarily mean that you were discriminated against. It's easy to rationalize and develop excuses when we ask ourselves such things as: Was my preparation adequate? Did I perform consistently? Did I follow through on tasks? Have I been a team player?

Ask yourself whether the company has some legitimate complaints about your performance, such as habitual tardiness, not putting in eight-hour days, or anything else your boss has reprimanded you about. He or she will usually document these conferences with memoranda to file. Management refers to this as "building a case." Later, if you are let go or held back, the company will produce these memos or conversation records to defend its actions.

Cases of poor performance have been built against workers in order to justify dismissal or lack of promotion even though the real motivation was racial bias. The best protection is good records and copies of your performance evaluations.

SHOULD YOU FIGHT?

If you decide you were dismissed or held back because of racism rather than forces in the marketplace, office politics, or poor performance, you have some tough decisions to make. It's your responsibility to blow the whistle if you feel you have been the victim of discrimination. But before you take such drastic action, explore the potential dangers and consequences and weigh them against what you might gain. It's generally easier to fight if you have lost a job; you have nothing to lose. Making waves about not getting a promotion, on the other hand, is a lot more risky.

In either case, though, proving bias can be difficult and disruptive. You could be stigmatized and labeled a troublemaker, and that could stop your career dead. Even if you get the promotion or keep the job, your enemies may find subtle ways to make your life miserable or undermine your new authority. And they may eventually drive you out.

Talking It Out

If, however, you have a strong case, you can go to management and tell them you feel you were discriminated against. This should be done amicably and rationally. But just saying you were discriminated against is not enough; you must give specific reasons. You must show not only that you are qualified but that the decision to fire you or not promote you was based on racial or cultural bias.

This starts with your immediate supervisor and may require going even higher if the issue is not resolved to your satisfaction. It's a little like someone saying you're guilty (in this case, lacking), and the burden of proving your innocence is on you. In addition to going to management, you should talk to the company's EEO officer (or, if the company is small, you may need to go to the nearest branch of the Equal Employment

Commission). If your case is strong, this can often lead to a quick resolution without formal action.

In the case of a missed promotion, talk to your boss and the EEO officer about your qualifications and strong interest in advancement, but don't attack or criticize. Even though you are not yet filing a formal EEO complaint, this puts management on notice that if they pass over you again, they could have problems.

Also, give your boss a chance to explain exactly why you were passed over. Then ask him or her what you can do to improve in those areas. This might include taking in-house training courses or extra credits at the local university or simply gaining more experience on the job.

Some may say that by taking your problem to your EEO officer, you're using your minority status as a way to coerce management into giving you a promotion or keeping you on the job. You're not. If you're qualified and are performing well, you should have the same opportunities as any other worker to climb the corporate ladder. That's what affirmative action is all about—trying to provide a level playing field where all workers have the chance to contribute and reap the rewards.

One note of caution before you go any further: Make sure you are right before filing a formal EEO complaint. This should never be done frivolously. And if you take the next step and decide to file a lawsuit, make doubly sure you are right, because it can have an impact on the rest of your career. It's unfortunate, but if you're discriminated against you must weight the consequences of whether to try to right the wrong. That, however, is the reality of our work environment.

Squaring Off and Surviving a Fight

If you don't get anywhere with informal discussions and decide to take formal action, you should start by filing a formal EEO complaint through the company's EEO office or the local office of the Equal Employment Opportunity Commission. Before doing this you should advise your supervisor of your intentions.

A representative from the commission will investigate the charges. Both you and the company will be asked to provide information. Although much of this will be written in the form of statements and in response to questionnaires, you will probably also be interviewed. After their fact-finding, it can be a matter of weeks or even several months before a decision is reached.

If you win, the company could be penalized and ordered to right the wrong. You will, however, probably be branded as a troublemaker. Not on paper, of course, but the label will be there. Your job will be safe, though, because most firms will not risk a lawsuit to force you out. The negative impact on your career at that company may very well depend on its size. Generally, the larger the organization, the less impact. Even if they win their EEO suit, however, most people eventually move on to other organizations.

Fighting dismissal, on the other hand, may involve filing not only an EEO complaint but a lawsuit to recover damages. A notice of your right to sue will be issued 180 days from the date your charge was filed. (You can request that it be issued earlier, but whether your request is granted is at the discretion of the EEOC.)

Before you hire a lawyer and file suit, you should know what you want: financial compensation, reinstatement, or a combination. A good lawyer can provide guidelines. Find one who specializes in this type of work, but never pay up front. Hire someone who will take the case on a contingency basis. That is, if they don't collect, you don't pay.

In the case of a lawsuit, most companies will eventually settle out of court. They are no more anxious to go to court or to receive negative publicity than you are. Your case won't be resolved overnight, though. You should be prepared to wait 6 to 18 months. In the meantime, you'll probably need to find another way to make ends meet.

When you apply for a new job, say you were laid off from your former position. Don't mention that you are in the process of suing your former employer unless you are specifically asked. This can be very delicate. Handle it that way.

Try to use friends and co-workers you trust for both verbal and written references. Even if your prospective employer contacts your last workplace, the vast majority of companies will only verify dates of employment, salary, and job titles. This is true even if the employee left under friendly circumstances. The reason is simple: Too many companies have been sued because someone in personnel hinted at a problem and cost a former employee a position with another organization. If your personal references check out, you will probably be okay.

THE LIMITS OF THE LAW

Where discrimination exists and can be proved, the government's power to act on the part of the complaining employee is strong. For example, if your boss blatantly singles you out for verbal abuse or exclusion from some activities or opportunities becasue of your race or culture, then you may have a basis for complaint. But things are not always what they seem. If the boss makes unflattering remarks to everyone in his or her group, you may have a difficult time proving discrimination. After all, you are receiving equal treatment (even if it is less than optimal).

> **Losing your job or missing out on a promotion doesn't necessarily mean you were discriminated against.**

It's in dealing with these more subtle forms of discrimination that the government is often powerless. The official position of a corporation may be equal opportunity, but organizations are made up of individuals. Consider some of the ways people and companies can, and do, discriminate.

George, a middle-aged white man, lives in Phoenix, Arizona, where he manages the financial group for a medium-sized electronics firm. Although he has been heard to complain about minorities, he will tell you he doesn't hate them. But there's no doubt they make him uneasy, and he feels threatened. He also suspects that they don't really share his values of hard work and going the extra step to get the job done.

George has a few minorities in his 25-person group, but he says emphatically, "I don't want them taking over the place." His solution is startlingly simple and almost impossible for the government to prosecute. When a resume comes in, George gives it his "minority scan." It works like this: He looks at where the applicant went to school. Is it a school that's predominantly made up of minorities? How about the applicant's name? Does it sound ethnic? How about professional affiliations? Does the applicant belong to an ethnic association?

While it is illegal, too often George's minority scan works. He knows the law, but he doesn't believe he is breaking it. His logic is simple. "I don't exclude minorities from my organization," he says. "I just believe I should have the right to control how many we have."

Fortunately, the world is not full of Georges. But they are out there. Government officials responsible for enforcing Title VII of the Equal Employment Act say that this type of subtle bias is extremely hard to detect and correct. "We have found a few cases with a 'smoking gun,'" says James H. Troy, director of the EEOC's Office of Program Operations. "One instance involved people who were doctoring applications. That is, they were putting code words on applications to flag minorities. These types of cases we can handle."

But if there is a lack of hard evidence, labor law experts say the Georges of the world get caught only when there is a clear pattern. For example, say a company operates in a metropolitan area where 30 percent of the population is minority. If that firm has few, if any, minorities, then they may be practicing unfair screening of applicants, or they may be slanting their recruiting efforts to exclude minorities.

Discrimination can be just as subtle on the job. Suppose you and three nonminority candidates are competing for a promotion to a managerial position. Information such as reports and business trend analyses may be conveniently withheld from you but not the nonminority candidates. When you go through the internal screening and interview process, you are going to be less informed and are not going to look as qualified as the others. Later, the company can say with all honesty that you weren't selected because one of the others was more qualified.

In such a case discrimination is almost impossible to prove. The same holds true when charges of discrimination become intertwined with poor performance.

YOUR SECRET WEAPON

Good records arm you against charges of inadequate performance. Virtually all companies conduct some type of formal annual or semiannual evaluation process, the vast majority of which are written. Usually you go over the highlights with your supervisor and have the opportunity to see what was checked off or written in the different performance-evaluation categories.

When you receive your evaluation, make sure it is accurate. Challenge anything that isn't. Avoid initialing or signing a performance review if it doesn't reflect what you have done. Discuss it thoroughly with your boss. Ask for suggestions on how to improve your performance or how to strengthen your chances for promotion. Keep a copy of the evaluation and a summary of your conversation with your manager.

The reason is simple. If you have amassed a file of at least satisfactory evaluations, it is hard for the company to say later that you weren't performing up to par.

Digging for the Truth

For over four years, Jonathan, a 42-year-old African American, worked with a large Boston consulting firm that provided technical services to the federal government. As a senior systems analyst, he worked with clients and provided a liaison between the company and the government. He also prepared technical reports and other products for the client.

Three weeks after his annual evaluation, he was fired. The official reason was that he was not performing at a level commensurate with his salary and experience. In his termination letter Jonathan's boss also hinted that the company could not afford a senior person in a job that could be filled by a more junior person. This translated into "You have not grown professionally." Jonathan's boss also stated that he had sent Jonathan's resume throughout the company, and no one wanted to pick him up.

Jonathan went home and reflected on what had happened. After a couple of days, he called the company's EEO officer and said he felt he had been unfairly treated. The officer was sympathetic but said he felt that there were no grounds for further action. Angry, Jonathan called a lawyer.

In his initial interview with the attorney, Jonathan stated his case and produced copies of four annual performance evaluations. They were all above average or outstanding. The lawyer started asking questions. What could have changed in less than a month since his last performance evaluation? Had he performed as required? Yes. Had he been reliable and punctual? Yes. Had he delivered quality work? Yes. Had he adhered to the company's dress code? Yes. Had anyone ever made racist remarks to him? Only the occasional ethnic joke, which he had shrugged off.

Frustrated, the lawyer dug deeper. What she uncovered was that Jonathan's client, a high-level government civil servant, had recently been transferred to another agency. This client, an African American, had been replaced by a white woman. In view of Jonathan's documented performance evaluations, the attorney decided that this had to be the deciding factor in the firing. She took the case and filed a request with the EEOC for a notice of the right to sue.

It was granted, and for almost a year it looked as though Jonathan and his former employer would meet in court. Six weeks before the court date, however, company officials approached the lawyer and offered to settle out of court. Jonathan received eleven months' back pay, an offer of reinstatement to a comparable position, reimbursement for legal costs, and a monetary settlement for his aggravation and inconvenience.

Wake-Up Call

For two years, Sylvia, a 25-year-old Hispanic, worked with a large Texas-based computer firm. She was part of a 20-person group of programmers, technical writers, and computer scientists. As a software engineer she handled the company's data base administration. She also performed verification and validation for new software development.

Sylvia was known for being habitually late, something Charles, her supervisor, brought to her attention on a fairly regular basis. He also wrote two short memos to file documenting the situation. He provided her with copies but never brought the matter to higher management. And his reprimands were never strongly worded.

After Charles's warnings, Sylvia made a special effort to arrive on time, but it never lasted more than a month or so.

Still, her work was good, and this was reflected in her performance reviews.

At the beginning of her third year with the company, the company began to consolidate operations. Charles resigned, and Sylvia found herself with a new boss who seemed ill at ease with the large number of Hispanics in the group. Although he was grouchy to most of the workers, he seemed to focus his contempt for Latinos on Sylvia in particular. However, this was never done in front of others.

When she looked back later, Sylvia recalled one incident in particular. After a lunch break during which Sylvia had a conversation in Spanish with one of her friends, her new boss told Sylvia that he thought people who lived in the United States should speak English. He hinted that if they didn't want to do this, they should go back where they came from.

He reserved his outright hostility until he called Sylvia on the carpet for her tardiness. Like Charles, he wrote memorandums to file, but his memos were scathing indictments of what he perceived as Sylvia's laziness and lack of responsibility. Sylvia would later swear that she had never seen these memos.

It's in dealing with more subtle forms of discrimination that the government is often powerless.

Sylvia realized that she could be in trouble. She began to take extra care that she worked eight-hour days. She also started keeping copies of her time sheets. Her firing came on a

Friday in the form of a letter, which referred to her poor-quality work and tardiness. Sylvia was stunned. Immediately, on the advice of an older colleague, she filed an EEO complaint.

During the investigation the boss produced not only his memos but Charles's as well. Based on circumstantial evidence, he also made a strong case for Sylvia's declining performance. For example, because of the extra work she inherited during the consolidation and reorganization, she was behind in her efforts to verify and validate new software programs. With the exception of time sheets, Sylvia had nothing to produce in her defense. Although her boss had shown his dislike for Hispanics, she had no concrete evidence to prove this.

Sylvia appealed to her former officemates to back her up and help substantiate that the boss disliked Hispanics. But, afraid of losing their jobs too, they refused. The government upheld the company's decision to terminate Sylvia's employment. She lost because she had no documented evidence of her boss's bias toward Hispanics in general and her specifically. While the EEOC acknowledged that she had kept records showing that she had worked full eight-hour days, it noted that a condition of employment was to work between the hours of 8 a.m. and 5 p.m. She had failed to do this.

Two Wrongs Make a Right

Charles, a 23-year-old African American, had a similar problem with a very different outcome. Charles worked in his insurance company's customer service department. His boss, a white man in his late 50s, was known for his ethnic jokes and slurs. Charles managed to stay out of his way, however, for his first few months on the job.

The trouble began when Charles started carpooling to work

with his friend Daniel, a young white professional who also worked in the department. The two young men had a tendency to arrive late for work, and Charles's boss began reprimanding Charles for his tardiness and writing memos to his personnel file.

Charles was planning his long Memorial Day weekend when the boss called him into the office and handed him a notice of termination. Charles calmly tried to talk to him but to no avail. He cleaned out his desk and went home. At Daniel's urging he called the district office of the EEOC and said he was fired because of his race. An investigation was launched.

In the end the EEOC upheld Charles's complaint, and he was reinstated. The EEOC found that while Charles had indeed failed to uphold a major condition of employment, he had also not received equal treatment. No memos to file were produced by the company regarding his co-worker Daniel's tardiness, yet the two men carpooled together—in effect keeping identical hours. This fact alone indicated discrimination because Daniel, a white man, had not suffered the same consequences for his lateness.

The difference between the cases of Charles and Sylvia is the issue of equal treatment for all employees. If you discharge a minority and another person is guilty of the same offense, the company has to show consistency. Had the company also fired Daniel, it might have won.

The Poor Performer

Simon's parents immigrated from Taiwan to California when he was 12 years old. The young Asian worked hard to learn the language and fit into his new environment. By the time he graduated from college with a degree in electrical engineering, he felt he had achieved those goals.

Simon was heavily recruited and finally joined an aerospace firm. He proved to be an excellent young engineer, and after a year and a half he was promoted. His responsibilities shifted from design to providing oversight to the efforts of other engineers. It was more than he was ready for. Soon he was being pressured from all sides to do better; everyone, it seemed, was angry with his performance. He was devastated when he was demoted. Up to that point, his life had been marked by success both in school and on the job.

Over the next couple of months he became angry, then angrier still when his old job went to a young white engineer who had risen through the company's management-training program. Simon talked to the company's affirmative action officer and decided to file a complaint. He acknowledged that he hadn't done a very good job in his brief role as a manager, but he claimed the company had discriminated against him by not preparing him for the job as they had his successor.

The government's finding was lengthy, but the bottom line was that company attorneys were successful. They showed that Simon had not been pressured, criticized, and ultimately demoted because he was a minority, but that he had simply done a poor job of managing the group. They further proved that the company had provided various management-training opportunities, but Simon had not participated in the seminars and workshops.

Simon lost because he failed to meet performance expectations. In this case, that was a personal responsibility.

It's What's on Top That Counts

When James graduated with a liberal arts degree, he knew he liked working with others but wasn't sure what he wanted to do. When a friend mentioned a management trainee opening at a large hotel chain, James decided to give it a try. He would start on the reception desk and eventually work his way through the other aspects of the business. He was told it was also an opportunity to travel.

After six months he started dating a young woman from Jamaica who also worked in the hotel, and a serious relationship developed. She introduced him to new food and new friends. Gradually James began to adopt many of the ways of his new social circle. He changed his hairstyle, letting it grow long and having it braided into cornrows. That's when the trouble started.

His manager immediately expressed disapproval. She pointed out that because James was on the front desk, it was important that he project the image the hotel wanted. James politely pointed out that he wore a suit and performed his duties in a professional manner and that his hairstyle was his personal business.

A feud developed, and James and his manager eventually stopped speaking altogether. The manager cut James's scheduled work time down from 40 hours a week to 32. When that didn't produce results, she made James work the dreaded night shift. James retaliated by filing an EEO complaint. During the investigation, the company didn't fire him but transferred him from the front desk to the back office, where he had no contact with the public. In the end the government upheld James's right to wear whatever hairstyle he wished, finding that he had not violated the company's stated dress code. Hairstyles weren't included as part of that code.

Even though he won, James left the company shortly after the government's decision. He felt the confrontation had destroyed the basis for an effective working relationship. In retrospect he admits that there had been room for compromise on both sides. He wishes he had explored this route before the conflict escalated. He says, "Technically I won, but I feel like I lost."

Of course, discrimination is only one of many problems that can lead to job upheaval. It's important to be prepared for such bumpy spots in your career; good planning and a positive attitude can carry you through.

Author's Note:
The material in this chapter is for information only and is not intended to replace professional legal advice. You should consult an EEO officer and an attorney before initiating legal action to fight job discrimination.

Chapter 10

CHANGING DIRECTIONS: MAKING THE RIGHT MOVES

People, personal goals, situations, industries, and companies change constantly. It can be chaotic. At best, you initiate and control change. At worst, change is forced on you.

Beyond being fired or laid off, there are a variety of reasons for wanting personal change. You're bored, frustrated, and want more challenge. You've acquired new skills you want to use. You don't like the work. You've become interested in another career. The list is endless.

No matter the reason, everyone faces some form of change at various stages in their careers. The secret is to make these transitions as smooth as possible.

YOU'RE FIRED!

Over the course of their careers, as many as one in four of all workers hear the words "You're fired!" or receive the dreaded pink slip, according to a survey conducted by Robert Half International, Inc., a nationwide recruiting firm. The initial shock of being fired, no matter the reason, can wound the deepest part of us. It can make us feel angry, guilty, frustrated, scared, or a little bit of each.

There are usually danger signs: being passed over for pay raises or promotions, having responsibilities taken away, being left out of corporate meetings, being shunned by your boss or co-workers, being demoted, or having perks taken away. These should have alerted you that trouble is brewing. But even with warning, being fired is usually like a cold shower.

The Emotional Toll

Although you may be well versed in the "mechanics" of finding another position after you've been sacked, you also need to be prepared to deal with the emotional strain.

For most of us, a job provides more than income; it's a cornerstone to our sense of worth and our identity. Seeing that cornerstone crumble can elicit a host of negative behaviors, from becoming hostile and engaging in a shouting match with the boss to quietly drowning in self-pity. But while depression, frustration, and anger are all normal emotions after a firing, you can't afford to dwell on them.

Sure, you're going to look back. Perhaps you made some mistakes. Sort them out and learn from them. But asking yourself over and over "Why didn't I do this?" or "Why didn't I see that?" is counterproductive. Don't become fixated on what happened; you can't change it. You can only take steps to ensure that past mistakes aren't repeated. You don't need guilt. What you need is hope and a plan. Never forget that there is a big difference between "taking responsibility" and "blaming yourself." You must do the former or you can't develop your career. The latter is merely self-destructive.

Even if you did your best, the reality is that hard work is not always going to pay off—and not just because of discrimination. Regardless of whether what happened to you was the result of a mistake on your part or due to outside influences beyond your control, learn from the experience and let it go.

Shake the shock and recover your balance. Take time to do something to cope with stress. Many people find long walks, jogging, or other forms of exercise helpful. Remember, you *will* work again. Action is often the best cure for the "canned blues." Don't be paralyzed by doubt. The longer you wait before you go after that first interview, the more convinced you'll be that you are unemployable.

STARTING OVER

Regardless of the reason, if you were wearing your parachute (as described in Chapter 8), you should be able to hit the ground running. If not, you need to take steps to get your search into high gear. (Review the job-hunt details in Chapter 3.)

Attitude is paramount during your search for a new job. Adopt the right mind-set. Think of this as a transition phase in your career, one that offers new opportunities and beginnings that can excite you and stir your imagination.

You Can't Score From the Bench

Don't be your own worst enemy. There are enough obstacles out there; you don't need to set up any more. Yet far too many minorities do just that. When your career hits a rough spot, remember:

- **Lack of opportunity** is a myth—regardless of economic conditions. As a minority, you should never believe you can't make it or that you will never succeed because there are no jobs out there. It's not true. You got a job once; you can do it again. And this time, with the advantage of experience and a strong network, the task should be much easier.

- **Overcoming pride** is essential. You need to ask others for help; that's what a network is for.
- **Anger** at former bosses or organizations is heavy baggage and reflects poorly on you. Others will know if you are carrying a grudge. Never let leftover feelings of hostility taint your search.
- **Guilt** for past mistakes changes nothing and can only lead to depression. Shrug it off and move on.
- **Fear of rejection or feeling inferior** is total nonsense. Nobody ever scores every time they shoot. It only takes one "Congratulations, you've got the job" to wipe out a month of hearing "Sorry, we can't use you."
- **Passing the buck** by expecting others to do your work only ensures that you won't get the job you want.
- **Great expectations** are fine for the long run, but right now you can't afford to be either unrealistic or unreasonable. You might have to make some short-term sacrifices, such as a pay cut or a less responsible position, to ultimately get where you are going.
- **Procrastination** is a career killer. You can't afford to hang around home daydreaming. No one is going to come looking for you. You have to get back out there today and start opening some doors.

Persistence Pays

Your next job is out there. Just ask Larry. After being laid off from a Rhode Island savings and loan when the organization collapsed, he applied to similar organizations throughout the Northeast. "I soon had enough rejection letters to wallpaper my den," he says. Undaunted, he broadened his search to include corporate finance departments and banks. He still failed to land an offer.

Puzzled, he took his resume and cover letters to a family friend who was a financial analyst with a Boston bank. The older man took one look at Larry's package and pointed out that it was too slanted toward his former business and didn't emphasize his transferable financial skills. Together they rewrote two versions—one aimed at the banking industry and another aimed at corporate financial operations. Within three weeks Larry received a solid offer from the financial division of a major fast-food chain.

Again, remember that being "axed" isn't just an ending; it's an opportunity to make a new beginning. That's how it worked out for Raymond.

When the 28-year-old Hispanic was fired from his hospital administration job in Los Angeles by a new chief administrator who felt threatened by Raymond's initiative, he looked for a similar position but had no success. Instead, he ended up finding a whole new career, managing a church group's efforts to help Mexican immigrants sort through their paperwork and find housing and jobs. "I never realized how miserable I was at the hospital," Raymond says. "I love this job. It's an opportunity to put my language and administrative skills to use for a community-oriented project."

THE GREAT ESCAPE

Perhaps your job is still secure, but you have a nagging feeling that you need a change. This is not just one of those restless days when you feel overworked and trapped, when you feel like going to lunch and never coming back. It's more deeply rooted. Don't ignore those feelings; find out what's causing them. Are you suffering from temporary frustration? Do you find yourself in a no-win situation? Do you need to rise above a plateau?

A good indicator is your performance review. An average appraisal may reflect that you're bored and stagnating or that your job doesn't match your skills, goals, or personality. It might also indicate that you lack the support or authority to get the job done.

If you decide you want a change, don't allow your dissatisfaction to get you fired. But don't just quit, either. Take advantage of the luxury of conducting a job search while you enjoy the security of already having one. Of course, you probably won't want your present employer to know you're doing this; use discretion.

Moving Sideways

You can scratch the itch for change in several ways. One is changing your environment without changing your company.

There are valid reasons for not leaving your company even if you find yourself in an unhappy work situation. They include company loyalty, job security, the promise that things will eventually get better, a sluggish economy, and the need to gain more work experience. But waiting can become a frustrating proposition unless you can find a way to deal with your dissatisfaction.

Perhaps the most practical way to escape a boring or dead-end job is to make a lateral move within your company. Many young professionals don't realize that trying to move up the ladder is only one way to manage a career. Lateral transfers may not bring increased earnings, but they can often provide new challenges and broaden your capabilities.

When Lianne found herself increasingly unhappy with her position as a technical writer, she looked around for other openings in her company. She decided to try for an opening at the customer-assistance desk. After all, she had written the computer user manuals and knew the systems. By moving sideways into customer assistance, she stayed at the same pay level but gained experience working with clients and sharpened her people skills.

After a year Lianne moved back to the writing group with renewed enthusiasm and newly acquired skills. She was eventually promoted to head the publications department.

> **Being "axed" isn't just an ending; it's an opportunity to make a new beginning.**

Here are some tips for successful in-house job changes:

- Know your organization's policies and procedures for a job change.
- Keep track of vacancies in your organization that might be a good fit for you.
- Be on the lookout for the right moment to make your move.

- Take advantage of any career-development services or company-sponsored educational opportunities offered by your company.

Redesign Your Job

Another option is to try to restructure your current job. Like most employees, you may not realize that your job isn't cast in concrete. You generally don't have to accept the position as a rigid set of tasks. Jobs should and do evolve over time. You can accelerate the process by looking for job changes that benefit not only you but the company as well. Study the overall organizational picture and try to develop changes that increase your power and control over your work. For example, you might start by demonstrating your ability to schedule your own work. Once you have established this precedent with your boss, you are in a position to start making changes in the actual tasks.

Moving On

Sometimes, leaving your company may be the only cure for your job dissatisfaction. Maybe you are ambitious, but your boss is only a couple of years older than you; your company's growth is sluggish and management doesn't seem aggressive enough to turn it around; your company is the target of a merger or buyout; or you're simply burned out and unable to muster any real enthusiasm for the job.

If you're considering leaving, you need to evaluate all the factors involved. Start by assessing your own performance. Ask yourself if you have really given 100 percent to your job. If not, try to figure out what has held you back. Can you change it?

Next, evaluate the company itself. Is it really challenging you? Do you have enough independence? Do people listen to your recommendations? Are you making the money you feel you deserve or need?

Finally, evaluate your goals. Have they changed? Are your priorities different? Has your lifestyle changed?

Review the answers and determine if you can resolve the problems without leaving. And if you do decide to leave, make sure you know what career options you want to pursue. And make sure you have the qualifications you need. Then you're ready to begin a new job search.

The Two-Year Itch

Young professionals, especially those in high-demand jobs, often start out their careers by job hopping for fun and profit. "I've had four jobs in four years," says Beverly, a software engineer in Chicago. "This is a relatively hot field. I don't want to settle for a 3 percent raise when I can move to another organization and make 15 percent for the change."

But as Gregory, a programmer in Seattle, discovered, staying on the job-hop track too long can hurt you. "I've had five jobs in seven years; now I'm somewhat overpriced," he says. The 29-year-old adds, "I'm not going anywhere at the moment. I've found out that many managers may indulge some hopping early on in your career, but when you have been around for a while, they expect some stability. They simply need to be able to count on some reasonable longevity from an individual. The reason is that it costs time and money to keep replacing staff members."

In certain industries where contracts or work changes hands frequently, job hopping may be more acceptable. This is especially true of companies in which most of the work is government-related. If a company loses a big competitive contract, then professionals from that organization tend to migrate to the firm that won it. Also, certain high-tech corridors tend to have a more mobile work force. In general, though, limit job hopping to the early part of your career, when you can explain it as "getting your feet wet."

CAREER TRANSITIONS

If your interests have changed or you simply selected a field that didn't turn out to be what you'd hoped, you may want to consider changing careers. Many professionals dream about it, but few ever make the leap. To deliberately seek any change takes courage and optimism—and that holds especially true if you are moving from one career to another. It can be financially risky and tough on your emotions. And the longer you wait, the more difficult it becomes.

A surprising number of people start down the wrong career path and continue along it for a lifetime because they are unsure how to change directions. You don't have to be one of them. First of all, accept that there is never going to be a convenient time to switch careers. Next, find out what you really want to do. (You can start by going back to Chapter 2 and re-evaluating your goals.)

Look at what you have become as a result of experience and desire. Identify other sides of yourself, including skills you haven't used for a while or that aren't the focus of your current position. If, for example, you're an accountant, on any given day you may have also been a sales manager, a marketing rep, customer service rep, and a trainer. Don't box yourself in by thinking in terms of your job title. See yourself as a resource available to others.

Planning the Change

After you are sure of what you want, make a list of the steps you must take to get there. Do you need more education? Where can you gain relevant experience for your new career? Volunteer work, for example, can be a great way to learn different skills and test new waters.

Also list any links between what you'd like to be doing and your current position. For instance, say you have a bachelor's degree in business, but you want to go into teaching. What course work is common to both professions? Determine what additional courses are required to make the switch.

Finally, consider your financial situation and family responsibilities. How will you survive this transition? Perhaps your spouse's salary is sufficient to carry you through. Or you may decide to work part time or as a temp while studying or gaining other experience.

A career change can't be hurried. Take it one step at a time, and develop a plan that addresses each issue. Here's how Kelly did it. She graduated at age 22 with a degree in biology and was offered a job in a food-testing laboratory. After a couple of years she decided it wasn't for her. She did some soul-searching and took some aptitude tests. Finally, she decided she wanted to become a nurse.

Kelly arranged to work part time at the lab and went back to school. After the first year, she started having money problems and increased her part-time hours without cutting her class load. As a result, she nearly flunked out of school. She didn't want to take out any student loans, so she quit school. But she didn't give up her dream.

She went back to work full time and saved every penny she could. She even started sharing her apartment to cut expenses. After a year she again cut her work schedule and re-enrolled in school.

Accept that there is never going to be a convenient time to switch careers.

This time she was successful. She quit her part-time job in the lab and started working 20 hours a week as a nursing assistant in a retirement home, gaining valuable experience. When she was 29, Kelly finally became a registered nurse.

Was it worth it? "You bet," she says. "It was a long haul, but I love what I'm doing. It saved me from a career I really didn't enjoy. And I'm starting to make top dollar."

Career changes can tax your commitment to the limit. You not only need to gain new skills, but you have to convince employers of your worth even though you lack relevant work experience. (One strategy that can help is using a functional rather than a chronological resume. See Chapter 4.)

Transitions are a normal part of career development and management. Everyone has faced, or will face, changes as they pursue their career goals. It doesn't mean you have failed or planned poorly. Whether the change is forced or planned, take it in stride. Be confident that you can overcome temporary setbacks or frustrations and achieve new success—and you will.

Chapter 11

PASSING IT ON

Many successful minorities have paved the way for your own achievements. Some, like Dr. Mae Jemison, the first African-American woman astronaut, have made strides for the whole world to see. Most, however, have been quiet pioneers: the first minority manager or executive at your corporation, for example.

Their precedents and examples have opened doors for you. But many of these individuals have gone one step further: They have made a conscious effort to extend a helping hand to other minorities.

You share this responsibility, and you don't have to wait until you reach the executive suite to start doing your part. You can start helping others as soon as you land your first job and increase your efforts as you build your career. And you can make a difference in myriad ways: participating in a formal mentoring program sponsored by the company, volunteering to tutor at local schools, or simply befriending a new minority employee. Everyone will benefit from your actions. If you volunteer to help students, you might inspire someone to build a foundation for success. If you help a new employee adjust to the workplace, you could be playing an important role in the development of a future executive.

Most of life's transitions can be eased by the wisdom of those who have gone before. You may have only been on the job for a year, but you have learned through observation and your fair share of mistakes. Pass along this knowledge.

Like your career, your role as part-time mentor, teacher, and guide will involve skills, sacrifices, and challenges. Here are some basics:

You can start helping others as soon as you land your first job.

- **Listen.** Don't project your own ambitions on others; recognize that they may have different goals. Sometimes, just serving as a sounding board can go a long way toward helping others.

- **Be a people coach.** Offer constructive criticism and realistic suggestions. If you see a new employee who is not dressing properly, tactfully point it out and offer suggestions. Or if a fellow employee is faced with difficult job issues, help him or her sort out the options.

- **Be willing to sacrifice some personal time.** It might mean giving up an evening to tutor at the local school or a lunch hour to counsel a co-worker.

- **Work to develop sincere, honest, and trustworthy relationships.**

- **Don't assume you have all the answers.** Make sure the advice you give is based on solid, reliable information. If you don't know what to advise, say so.

- **Be prepared to help shoulder occasional failures.** When you become a mentor, those you help will sometimes make mistakes or fail. As a mentor, you have a responsibility to share not only their successes but their setbacks too.

- **Know when to let go.** Don't try to continue advising a person who no longer wants or needs your help.
- **Value community service.** Whenever possible, extend your support beyond the workplace.

Few of us are so busy that we can't touch at least one other life. Take the initiative and make a difference for other minorities. By giving back you will gain.

Final Thoughts

Recent trends and changes make today's workplace an exciting environment. And change always means opportunities to those who are prepared. Successful career management requires a lifetime of balance, flexibility, and adjustment. It's never too early or too late in your career for planning and personal improvement. That's why everyone should have at least a three-year plan and always be in year one of that plan.

Build on the opportunities being offered by the increased emphasis on cultural diversity. Remember the fundamentals:

- know your environment
- establish a reputation for reliability, quality, and integrity
- never stop learning
- always look ahead

As you enter the workplace and face the future, never confuse *job* with *career.* Jobs belong to companies. If you leave your job, someone will replace you. Your career, though, belongs to you. It's shaped by your unique blend of technical and people skills, your knowledge, and your personality. It's the vehicle that will carry you through your professional life.

Appendix

SELECTED MINORITY ORGANIZATIONS

This listing of selected minority associations, groups, and organizations is not intended to be all-inclusive but rather representative of the types of support and information sources available. Publications that offer a more complete guide to minority organizations can be found at the end of this list.

Affirmative Action Register
8356 Olive Blvd.
St. Louis, MO 63132
314-991-1335

Runs ads aimed at minority, female, and handicapped applicants.

American Association for Affirmative Action
11 E. Hubbard St.
Chicago, IL 60611
312-329-2512

Works to implement national affirmative action and EEO policies, establish ethical standards for professionals, and promote professional growth. Most members are EEO officers.

American Association for the Advancement of Science
Office of Opportunities in Science
1333 H St., NW
Washington, DC 20005
202-326-6670

Works to increase the types of opportunities available, provides information, and works with other related organizations.

American Association of School Administrators
1801 North Moore St.
Arlington, VA 22209
703-528-0700

The association's Office of Minority Affairs represents the special concerns of minority members.

American Consulting Engineers
1015 15th St., NW
Washington, DC 20005
202-347-7474

Comprised of consulting engineering firms in private practice. Conducts professional development and other programs.

American Counseling Association
The Human Rights Committee
5999 Stevenson Ave.
Alexandria, VA 22304
703-823-9800

Concerned with cultural diversity in the workplace.

American Planning Association
1776 Massachusetts Ave., NW, Suite 400
Washington, DC 20036
202-872-0611

Professional public and private planners and educators involved in urban and rural development. Association provides professional services, publications, and a resume service.

American Society for Training and Development
1640 King St.
Alexandria, VA 22313
703-683-8100

Professional association of training officers. Offers a Minority Network dedicated to providing support for professional development of minorities within ASTD.

Association of Cuban Civic Engineers
3383 NW 7th St., Suite 205
Miami, FL 33125
305-649-7429

Professional association of Hispanic engineers.

Association of Minority Health Profession Schools
711 Second St., NE, Suite 200
Washington, DC 20002
202-544-7499

Among its aims is increasing the number of African Americans in health care fields.

BAYNET
1900 Powell St., Suite 200
Emoryville, CA 94608
510-450-1055

Regional African American professional group. Provides career networking opportunities for over 2,000 members.

Black Collegian
1240 South Broad St.
New Orleans, LA 70125
504-821-5694

In addition to its magazine, sponsors job fairs and operates a resume service to help new graduates find employment.

Black Data Processing Associates
P.O. Box 7466

Philadelphia, PA 19101

Gathers and shares information processing knowledge and business expertise to increase career potential of minorities in the field. Conducts professional seminars and workshops.

Black Human Resources Network
1900 L St., NW, Suite 500
Washington, DC 20036
202-775-1669

Professional network of human resources specialists.

Blacks in Government
1820 11th St., NW
Washington, DC 20001
202-667-3280

National nonprofit organization concerned about work-related issues, with membership composed of all levels of federal, state, and local governments.

Career Communications Group
729 East Pratt St., Suite 504
Baltimore, MD 21202
410-244-7101

Publishes U.S. Black Engineer, Hispanic Engineer, *and* Black Professional *magazines. Also provides a computerized resume service for corporations seeking minority engineers.*

Coalition of Hispanic American Women
8572 SW 8th St.
Miami, FL 33144
305-262-0060

Includes scholarships, seminars, and professional and leadership development.

Council on Career Development for Minorities
1341 W. Mockingbird Lane, Suite 412-E
Dallas, TX 75247
214-631-3677
Works to heighten awareness and employability of minority college students and to improve career counseling and referral services offered to them.

Hispanic Data
c/o Hispanic Business
360 S. Hope Ave., Suite 300C
Santa Barbara, CA 93105
805-682-5843

Links Hispanic professionals with employers. Networks with over 200 colleges and over 100 professional organizations.

Hispanic Leadership Program
621 South Virgil Ave.
Los Angeles, CA 90005
213-736-1304

Provides management training to help Hispanics advance in both the public and private sectors.

INROADS
1221 Locust St., Suite 800
St. Louis, MO 63103
314-241-7330

Finds business internships for talented minority youth to prepare them for corporate and community leadership.

THE MINORITY CAREER GUIDE

Japan America Society of Southern California
505 S. Flower St.
Los Angeles, CA 90071
213-627-6217

Seeks to help Japanese and Americans achieve a better under-standing of each other.

Korean Scientists and Engineers Association in America
6261 Executive Blvd.
Rockville, MD 20852
301-984-7048

Links interests of scientists and engineers; works for closer relationships between Korea and the U.S.

Latin American Professional Women's Association
Box 31532
Los Angeles, CA 90031
213-227-9060

Promotes leadership development.

Minority Exploration Committee on Careers Associated
P.O. Box 450
New Brunswick, NJ 08903
908-932-0699

Sponsors career expos to link minority candidates with employers.

Minority Health Professions Foundation
8401 Colesville Rd., Suite 303
Silver Spring, MD 20910
301-565-9161

*Promotes educational and career opportunities for minority
students enrolled in member institutions.*

National Association of Asian American Certified Public Accountants

1 Embarcadero Ctr.
San Francisco, CA 94111
415-433-6396

*Professional association that seeks to address special concerns
and help with employment.*

National Association of Black Accountants, Inc.

220 I St., NE, Suite 150
Washington, DC 20002
202-546-6222

Provides professional information for members.

National Association of Black Women Attorneys

3711 Macomb St., NW
Washington, DC 20016
202-966-9691

Provides networking opportunities.

National Association of Negro Business and Professional Women's Clubs

1806 New Hampshire Ave.
Washington, DC 20009
202-483-4206

*Seeks to strengthen ties among African-American professional
women. Assists in career planning.*

National Association of Urban Bankers

1010 Wayne Ave., Suite 1210

Silver Spring, MD 20910-5600
301-589-2141

Offers information and sponsors programs to further careers of minority bankers and financial services professionals.

National Black M.B.A. Association
180 N. Michigan Ave., Suite 1515
Chicago, IL 60601
312-236-2622

Concerned with the role of African Americans who hold M.B.A. degrees. Encourages continuing education and assists students preparing to enter the business world.

National Black Nurses' Association, Inc.
1012 10th St., NW
Washington, DC 20001-4492
202-393-6870

Helps to enhance opportunities for minority nurses.

National Institute for Professional Development
Project Uplift
P.O. Drawer 30246
Albuquerque, NM 87110
505-265-4464

Concerned with multicultural education, professional development, and training systems. Sponsors a career expo and job fair aimed at Hispanics.

National Minority Faculty Identification Program
c/o Director of Institutional Research
Southwestern University
Georgetown, TX 78626

512-863-1220

Offers prospective employers a list of minority candidates for university teaching positions.

National Network of Minority Women in Science

c/o AAAS Office of Opportunities in Science
1333 H St., NW
Washington, DC 20005
202-326-6677

Works to increase number of minority women in science; offers placement services.

National Society of Black Engineers

344 1454 Duke St.
Alexandria, VA 22314
703-549-2207

Helps prepare engineering and science students for professional careers.

National Technical Association

P.O. Box 27787
Washington, DC 20038
202-829-6100

Focuses on professional opportunities and career advancement in science; offers placement services for members.

Society of Hispanic Professional Engineers

5400 East Olympic Blvd., Suite 306
Los Angeles, CA 90022
213-725-3970

Maintains a job referral file and provides legal and professional development services for its members.

U.S. Commission on Civil Rights
1121 Vermont Ave., NW
Washington, DC 20425
202-376-8177
Enforces civil rights legislation and provides oversight and coordination of all federal regulations, practices, and policies affecting equal employment opportunity.

U.S. Equal Employment Opportunity Commission
1801 L St., NW
Washington, DC 20507
202-663-4900
Maintains regional and district offices throughout the country.

OTHER USEFUL ORGANIZATIONS

National Employment Lawyers Association
535 Pacific Ave.
San Francisco, CA 94133
415-397-6335
Professional association of lawyers who represent individuals in cases of discrimination, wrongful termination, and other employee matters. Good resource for locating legal help.

Toastmasters International
P.O. Box 9052
Mission Viejo, CA 92690-7052
714-858-8255
Over 7,000 clubs around the country. Programs help individuals develop communications and leadership skills.

MAGAZINES

Black Careers
P.O. Box 8214
Philadelphia, PA 19101
215-387-1600

Bimonthly for high school seniors, college students and gradu-ates, and high school and college counselors.

Black Collegian
1240 South Broad St.
New Orleans, LA 70125
504-821-5694

Published bimonthly during the school year; provides career information for students and recent graduates.

Black Professional
Career Communications Group
729 East Pratt St., Suite 504
Baltimore, MD 21202
410-244-7101

For students and young professionals; offers career advice and profiles of successful African Americans.

Direct Aim
Communications Publishing Group
250 Mark Twain Tower
106 W. 11th St.
Kansas City, MO 64105-1806
816-221-4404

Biannual focusing on career possibilities and skill enhance-ment for young African Americans and Hispanics.

Equal Opportunity
150 Motor Pkwy., Suite 420
Hauppauge, NY 11788-5145
516-273-0066

Recruitment magazine for minority college graduates, sponsored by Equal Opportunity Publications.

Graduating Engineer Minorities Issue
Peterson's/COG Publishing Group
16030 Ventura Blvd., Suite 560
Encino, CA 91436
818-789-5293

Biannual with career advice for African American, Hispanic, and American Indian engineers.

Graduating Nurse Minorities Issue
(see address under *Graduating Engineer Minorities Issue*)
Annual with career information and opportunities for entry-level nurses and graduating RNs.

Hispanic Engineer
(see address under *Black Professional*)

Quarterly offering college students and professionals career advice and profiles of successful Hispanics.

Hispanic Magazine
Hispanic Publishing Corporation
111 Massachusetts Ave., NW, Suite 410
Washington, D.C. 20001
202-682-3000

General editorial magazine covering Hispanic interests.

Minority Engineer
(see address under *Equal Opportunity)*

Sponsored by Equal Opportunity Publications; free to eligible minority engineers and engineering students.

Minority MBA
*(*see address under *Graduating Engineer Minorities Issue)*

Annual providing career information and advice for African American and Hispanic graduate business students.

Minority Nurse Professional
(see address under *Graduating Engineer Minorities Issue*)

Annual focusing on challenges and opportunities for young nurses.

Science and Engineering Horizons Minority Edition
(see address under *Graduating Engineer Minorities Issue*)
Annual providing technical students with career information.

U.S. Black Engineer
Career Communications Group
729 East Pratt St., Suite 504
Baltimore, MD 21202
410-244-7101

Offers college students and young professionals career advice and profiles of successful African Americans.

MINORITY ORGANIZATION RESOURCES

These publications, available in most libraries, list professional associations and cultural and special-interest organizations.

Asian Americans Information Directory
Black Americans Information Directory
Hispanic Americans Information Directory
Gale Research, Inc.
835 Penobscot Bldg.
Detroit, MI 48226-4094

Governing Bodies of Federally Recognized Indian Groups
Bureau of Indian Affairs
U.S. Department of the Interior
Washington, DC 20240

Guide to Black Organizations/
Guide to Hispanic Organizations
Public Affairs Dept., Philip Morris Ltd.
100 Park Ave.
New York, NY 10017

Minority Organizations: A National Directory
Garrett Park Press
Box 190
Garrett Park, MD 20896

Index

About the Authors

Michael F. Kastre, a writer and consultant, is the author of over 100 magazine and newspaper articles for such publications as *The National Business Employment Weekly, US Black Engineer,* and *Hispanic Engineer.* He has also been a human resources manager at a major Washington, D.C., consulting firm, where he got a behind-the-scenes look at corporate hiring practices, employee policies, and office politics. For the past six years Mr. Kastre has specialized in writing about career management issues for minorities.

A native of Colombia, co-author Nydia Rodriguez Kastre has lived in the United States for 17 years and has served in a variety of business roles, including management, sales, and staff positions. For 12 years she worked as a bilingual secretary for a large Washington, D.C., international organization. She later founded a manufacturing company and served as both president and marketing director. Ms. Kastre, who also holds a degree in interior design, has had extensive first-hand experience with minority workplace issues.

Co-author Alfred G. Edwards has worked for over 21 years as a professional corporate services consultant. During his career he has managed the development of information systems; provided financial and management services to government programs; and managed a multimillion-dollar operations center for a major consulting firm. A graduate of Howard University, Mr. Edwards is currently a program management consultant to the federal government and president of a gourmet coffee and food establishment.